Pot Luck

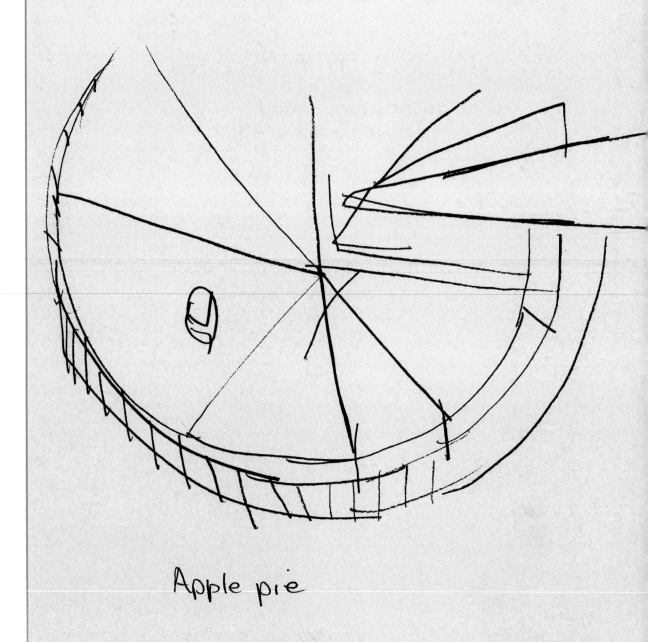

Apple pie

Drawing by one of the pupils of the Autistic Unit at Oak Lodge School

nife

Pot Luck

Recipes from the Stars

in aid of the Autistic Unit,
Oak Lodge School

Compiled by Caroline Esdaile

WITH A FOREWORD BY ANNIE BELL

Kyle Cathie Limited

First published in Great Britain in 1995 by
Kyle Cathie Limited
20 Vauxhall Bridge Road London SW1V 2SA

ISBN 1 85626 184 0

A Cataloguing in Publication record for this title
is available from the British Library.

Designed by Roger Walker/Graham Harmer
Edited by Caroline Taggart and Helen Dore
Printed in Spain by Gráficas Reunidas, Madrid

Contents

Foreword

The children in the autistic unit at Oak Lodge School in East Finchley, North London, are big, healthy and strong. It is striking how beautiful they are. Looking at a group of them having a drink and biscuit mid-morning, sitting around a table, it could be any group of primary school children. But then you notice the silence. Normal children would be chattering to each other, fooling around, whispering and giggling. It's not that these children can't talk. Many of them can, but they sit ignoring each other, oblivious to their neighbours.

Autism is a condition shrouded in misconception. If you mention it to someone, quite likely they will conjure in their mind a picture of a child or adult sufferer they have seen on a TV programme, which will have formed their image of the condition. For myself, before visiting Oak Lodge School, I envisaged a child unable to communicate with the outside world, whose frustration was inwardly directed, making him aggressive and self-destructive.

The first thing I learned was that there is no norm. Every child is different, and autism covers the entire spectrum of capabilities from normal and above learning capacity to severe learning difficulties. Likewise, while some of the children can be aggressive, others are quiet and introverted and will sit all day long without doing anything unless you motivate them.

There are three criteria for diagnosing a child as autistic. One is inappropriate social behaviour. These children are not bound by normal social mores, and cannot relate to what other people are feeling and thinking. In the worst cases there are parents who are literally imprisoned and cannot leave their child to visit the postbox. A child may hug or smack a complete stranger, or run up to another child and steal its ice-cream. Socially they stick out, even the very bright ones.

The second criterion is a resistance to change. Altering a routine can bring on sheer terror. If a different route to school is taken, a child may get very upset. There is a reliance on things always being the same.

The third criterion is ritualistic, obsessive behaviour. Where a normal child might play with a toy for five minutes and then grow bored and want a change, an autistic child may be immersed in turning the same pages of a book for an hour, and again become very upset if you try to stop it.

It is worth mentioning that many other children can display one or other autistic feature without being classified as autistic.

Parental involvement is very much a feature at Oak Lodge, and it was during a parent support meeting that the idea of producing a cookbook was suggested. Oak Lodge, like most normal schools, suffered a staffing cut two years ago; local education authorities are increasingly short of money, and having to rely on raising their own funds.

The money made by this book will go towards individual music therapy. This took some years to introduce into the curriculum, and the borough is not able to fund it, so money is desperately needed in order to continue with the programme.

Caroline Esdaile, the mother of a child at the unit, and Johanna Ruggeri, head of the department, have both been overwhelmed by the response to their request for support from the well-known and busy people who have contributed to this book. But without Caroline and Johanna's dedication it certainly could not have come about.

As a collection of recipes this is a wonderful hotchpotch ranging from Rowan Atkinson's 'Mr Bean's Beans on Toast', John Cleese's 'Breakfast Cornflakes', Dawn French's 'Three Mars Bar Fondue', to erudite contributions from Anton Mosimann, Delia Smith and Marco Pierre White. In fact, this is the most idiosyncratic, fun and interesting cookery book I have seen in a long time.

Annie Bell
March 1995

Foreword

More About Oak Lodge School

Oak Lodge is a school for children with moderate learning difficulties. There are about a hundred pupils aged from three and a half to eleven. Attached to the school there is a small unit for autistic children which currently has twelve pupils. The children need to be in a very small, structured group with a high staff-to-pupil ration, so for every three or four children within the department there will be two staff.

The school feels it is essential to intervene early in an autistic child's development, otherwise obsessional and ritualistic behaviour becomes ingrained. It is possible to redirect such tendencies, and there are success stories of children being integrated back into mainstream school at a later age.

One child, for instance, who arrived at the school aged three and a half with marked problems, existing in his own little world, has now been at a normal school for four years, even coping with the transition to secondary school. He is still autistic – this cannot be cured – but he is able to cope and can socialise with other children. In fact, with an obsessional aptitude for football, he is something of a hero among his peers.

It is not necessarily the aim to integrate every child back into mainstream schooling, but the children do improve with specialised care, and a huge difference can be made to their quality of life. The skills the children acquire within the unit go far beyond the national curriculum. It is a life training: exposing them to new experiences, helping them through, taking them to a new situation again and again until they feel confident.

Introduction

The headmistress of the nursery school Jonathan attended summoned my husband and me into her office and said, 'There is something very different about your little boy.' Jonathan was almost three. This conversation set us on a journey full of twists and turns, chasms and obstructions with a destination that was far from clear. It took another three years for Jonathan to be described as having autistic features, thus qualifying him for statementing as a child with special educational needs.

The intervening years should have been the happiest and most carefree of all our lives. Instead our family life was fraught with fear and anxiety. Jonathan could not be educated in mainstream schools. We tried to educate him at home, but we were desperate to find a school which would both value and help him.

Then came Oak Lodge.

Oak Lodge has a Unit for Autistic Children which is part of a school for pupils with moderate learning difficulties. Having identified the school, we had to wait a year before a place became available. But once he was there, Jonathan was at last provided with a secure, happy and structured environment. Johanna Ruggeri and her team of dedicated and inspired staff reduced the world and the business of learning into small, comprehensible stages. As parents we were always welcome at the school. We met other parents. Over a cup of coffee and a biscuit we shared our hopes and aspirations for our children; we supported each other. We were even able to laugh as we swapped stories. We were no longer alone.

However difficult the day has been and however many temper tantrums Jonathan may have experienced, the magic words 'dinner is ready' will bring him tearing to the table, where he will sit with his family and eat with relish.

Autism prevents Jonathan from finding the right words; it makes him overreact or not react at all. It makes him angry enough to break plates and very often impulsive enough to go up to strangers and hold their hands.

Yet Jonathan, and many children like him, comprehend so much. He sees life differently from you and me, and yet he feels deeply. Often he climbs the tallest tree and watches his younger brother playing football in the garden with friends. It is peaceful and he is in control. Unlike his

brother and sister, Jonathan has not acquired the conventional skills needed to form relationships.

Food is a universal language which forges a link between autistic children and the world outside. Jonatahn enjoys a good meal and is able to share this pleasurable experience with others; it is a time when he consolidates a bond with me and my husband, and his brother and sister. This is why a cookbook seemed an appropriate way of raising money to help his school.

I wrote to people who have the gift of communicating, be it by political thought, art, laughter or spiritual guidance, to see what food they enjoyed. *Pot Luck* began to take shape.

I explained to our potential contributors the need to perpetuate a Music Therapy Department at Oak Lodge. Music permeates all barriers. It is invaluable in the alleviation of the most traumatic of autistic symptoms. Tension, fear and anxiety can be expressed for the first time. Locked up emotions are revealed to trained therapists, leaving the child calmer and more secure. Often music facilitates elusive speech and helps children to accept periods of silence.

Matthew Fort, Food and Wine Editor of the *Guardian*, commented, 'Everyone should buy this book, not just because it contains stimulating and delicious recipes, but also because it will help Oak Lodge carry on its wonderful work.' Many others echoed these sentiments.

Many autistic children are sensitive, intelligent and gifted. They are a great source of joy to their families. A tremendous effort of will is needed to allow these special children to attain their full potential. Investment in education when they are young will help to prevent years of dependency and disillusion.

I was very moved by the numerous letter of goodwill and encouragement I received, especially by the blessing of His Holiness the Pope and other spiritual leaders. There are many cherished messages, even some from people who felt unable to contribute; in addition to those whose favourite recipes appear in the book I would particularly like to mention Kenneth Branagh, Jilly Cooper, Nigel Dempster, Lady Antonia Fraser, Sir Jeremy Isaacs, Sir Tim Rice and Zoe Wanamaker.

I do not know how Jonathan will develop, whether he will ever have a job, a family of his own, the many things that we all take for granted. But I do have a certain peace of mind knowing that at the end of a long, hard struggle he will have had the best education he could possibly have had and the very best of opportunities. As you browse through *Pot Luck* and relish the many exciting recipes, know that you have helped another autistic child and his or her parents to charter that most difficult of journeys. Thank you.

Introduction

Acknowledgements

The author and publishers would like to thank the following for permission to reproduce photographs in this book:

p. vi   Paul Fayman, styled by Vijay Patel of Daisy Chain Florists, London, W. 1.
p. 7 and p. 141 Michelle Garrett
p. 9 Julie Dixon
p. 15 and p.33 Iain Bagwell
p. 25, p. 53 and p. 103 Victor Albrow
p. 43 Peter Knab, styled by Diana Knab and with food preparation by Caroline Liddell
p. 132 Basil Pao

The jacket photograph is of Sue Lawrence's Sun-dried Tomato Risotto (see page 72).

Other photographs, illustrations and logos kindly given by the contributors. Our grateful thanks to you all.

Soups
&
Starters

Carrot and Sweet Potato Soup

Sweat the vegetables in the oil in a large saucepan until soft but not browned. Add the stock and orange juice. Simmer for 30 minutes without boiling.

Liquidize until smooth, then return to the rinsed-out pan. Add the milk and reheat gently without boiling. If the soup is too thick, add more stock.

Season to taste with salt and pepper and serve sprinkled with the coriander.

1 onion, finely chopped
3 large carrots, finely chopped
1 large sweet potato, finely chopped
1 tablespoon olive oil
300 ml/10 fl oz vegetable stock
300 ml/10 fl oz orange juice
300 ml/10 fl oz milk
1 tablespoon chopped fresh coriander

SIR GEORGE PINKER

Watercress Cream Soup

Melt the butter in a thick-based saucepan, then add the prepared leeks, potatoes and watercress and stir them around so that they are coated with the melted butter. Add some salt, cover with a lid and let the vegetables sweat over a low heat for about 20 minutes, giving the mixture a stir about halfway through.

After that, add the stock (or water), bring to simmering point, covered, for a further 10 to 15 minutes or until the vegetables are quite tender. Remove from the heat and when cool liquidize the soup but not too vigorously. Return the soup to the saucepan, stir in the cream, season to taste and reheat gently. When serving, garnish each bowl with a watercress sprig.

© Delia Smith 1994; recipe reproduced from Delia Smith's Complete Illustrated Cookery Course, published by BBC Books

2 bunches of watercress, destalked and chopped (reserve 4 sprigs for garnishing)
The white parts of 3 large leeks (about 450 g/1 lb), washed and chopped
2 medium potatoes, peeled and chopped
50 g/2 oz butter
850 ml/1½ pints very light chicken stock or water
150 ml/5 fl oz double cream
salt and freshly milled black pepper

To garnish
sprigs of watercress

Green Bean Soup

SERVES 4

450g/1lb green (shap) round
   beans
570ml/1 pint milk
1 tablespoon cornflour
$^1/_2$ carton sour cream
juice of half a lemon
salt and white pepper

*B*arely cover beans with boiling salted water and boil under just tender.

Slake cornflour with cold milk. Add to beans in their water and bring to the boil, stirring constantly. Season to taste.

When cool, add sour cream and lemon juice to taste.

SALLY GUNNELL

Leek and Potato Soup

675g/1$^1/_2$ lb small leeks
a little olive oil or butter
850ml/1$^1/_2$ pints water
2 chicken stock cubes
2 small potatoes, thinly sliced
a little double cream
salt and freshly ground black
   pepper
freshly grated nutmeg

*W*ash the leeks and cut them into small pieces. Cook them in the oil or butter in a large saucepan for about 3 minutes over a low heat. Do not brown.

Add the water and stock cubes and the potatoes. Cook until the leeks and potatoes are tender.

Liquidize and pass through a fine sieve. Return to the rinsed-out pan and add salt, pepper and nutmeg to taste. Heat through gently.

Just before serving add a little cream.

It is difficult to give precise quantities for this recipe. It needs to be made once then changed to suit your own taste with more leeks or less stock cube, etc. The potatoes are used as a thickener, so add enough to get the consistency you want.

This is one of my favourites, wonderful in the winter after a training session.

Good luck with your recipe book – I hope it raises lots of money for your very worthwhile cause.

Sally Gunnell

Soups & Starters

Sort of Lockshen Soup

SERVES 4

*B*ung a chicken into a saucepan of boiling water and add 1 large onion. Also bung in the chicken giblets and feet minus toenails, if you're not squeamish and if the butcher keeps the feet (which most don't). Use only free-range chook, they have better legs.

Simmer for about 1 hour, then allow the chicken to cool in the liquid.

When the chicken is cold, drain, reserving the liquid, and put into the refrigerator. Next day you can skim off the luvverly chicken fat, also known as schmalz, which is delicious on the famous chopped liver or even spread on bread as a sort of Jewish bread and dripping.

Chop up all sorts of root vegetables – carrot, turnip, swede, parsnip – and celery and onion and cook until tender in a pan of boiling water. Add the reserved chicken cooking liquid and season to taste. I add, according to whim, basil, parsley, mixed herbs, tomato purée, bouillon cubes – you know, a bissel dis a bissel dat, till it tastes just right.

When ready for the big nosh-up shred a generous portion of chicken into each soup bowl and cook vermicelli (Italian for lockshen noodles) according to the instructions on the packet.

This will cure most minor ailments, and quite a few major ones too. Autism I'm not sure but it can't do any harm.

Bon Appetit.

Best Wishes to all at OAK LODGE SCHOOL Carry on the good work Warren Mitchell

The Peasant Soup of Capri

SERVES 6

3 large peppers: red, green and yellow

2 large courgettes

8 small new potatoes

1 medium onion

3 medium garlic cloves

2 medium carrots

1 x 400 g/14 oz can of Italian tomatoes

85 ml/3 fl oz good olive oil

6–8 fresh basil leaves

1 teaspoon dried oregano

salt and freshly ground black pepper

1 medium aubergine

additional oil for frying the aubergine

*W*ash, core and de-seed the peppers and cut into rough segments about 1 cm/¹/₂ in wide. Wash and slice the courgettes into 5 mm/¹/₄ in rings and scrub the small potatoes. Peel and cut the onion into fine rings. Finely chop the garlic. Wash and scrub the carrots and slice them into 5 mm/¹/₄ in rings.

Place all the vegetables in a large saucepan and add the tomatoes, roughly chopped, with their juice. Pour in the oil and add the basil and oregano. Season to taste with salt and pepper. Cover and simmer for 30 minutes, stirring the mixture occasionally.

Meanwhile, wash the aubergines and cut them into small cubes. Fry in oil until golden, drain and set aside.

When the vegetables are ready, add the aubergine cubes, mix well, cover the pan and simmer for a further 10 minutes.

Allow to cool, but aim at serving this dish in large soup plates, just warm enough to appreciate the different vegetable flavours.

Soups & Starters

Lentil Soup

SERVES 4–6

Put the lentils into a saucepan with the stock. Add the onion, tomato and garlic and simmer for 30–45 minutes or until the lentils are soft.

Liquidize (or not if a more chunky soup is required) and return to the pan. Add the cumin and season to taste with salt and pepper. Heat through and just before serving add a squeeze of lemon juice.

225 g/8 oz split red lentils
1.2 litres/2 pints chicken stock
1 onion, chopped
1 tomato, sliced
2 garlic cloves, crushed
1 teaspoon ground cumin
salt and freshly ground black
  pepper
1 lemon

GLENDA JACKSON, M.P.

HOUSE OF COMMONS
LONDON SW1A 0AA
071-219 4008

July 19th.

Dear Mrs. Erdaile,
    Good luck with the
book & much love to
all the children.
    Best wishes,
    Glenda Jackson.

Potted Shrimps

SERVES 4

1 schooner of medium dry
  sherry

175 g/6 oz button mushrooms,
  chopped

a pinch of nutmeg, ground mace
  or similar spice to confuse
  your guests!

225 g/8 oz potted shrimps,
  thoroughly defrosted

4 slices of toast, crusts removed

*T*his is probably the simplest recipe ever for a delicious starter or a savoury, but do make sure you have defrosted the potted shrimps before you make it otherwise they go leathery. Don't tell your guests you made it in two minutes flat!

Put the sherry into a frying pan and add the mushrooms and your choice of spice. Bring to the boil, then simmer for about 1 minute. Add the potted shrimps (minus the butter if health conscious) and bring back to the boil. Serve immediately on dry toast.

Soups & Starters

Special Prawn Cocktail

SERVES 4

Make the sauce: mix the mayonnaise with the tomato ketchup to give it a pale pink colour. Mix in a dash of Worcestershire sauce or wine and add the garlic if used.

Arrange the prawns in 4 individual dishes on a bed of lettuce and cucumber slices and top with sauce. Cover with clingfilm and chill in the refrigerator for 1 hour before serving.

Scoop the melon into balls or cut into 1 cm/$\frac{1}{2}$ in cubes and add to the prawn cocktail 15 minutes before serving. Return to the refrigerator.

Serve garnished with lemon wedges.

Note: celery pieces may be used instead of melon.

200 g/7 oz peeled prawns
2 lettuce hearts, shredded
$\frac{1}{2}$ cucumber, thinly sliced
1 small melon
1 lemon, cut into wedges

For the sauce
2 tablespoons mayonnaise
1 teaspoon tomato ketchup
Worcestershire sauce or dry
    white wine
1 garlic clove, crushed (optional)

*Lots of luv,
Cilla
xx*

Marinade de Légumes à l'Italienne

SERVES 4

*A*n interpretation of a traditional Italian dish made with marinated vegetables.

1 medium firm, ripe aubergine
salt and freshly ground black
   pepper
150 ml/5 fl oz olive oil
2 red peppers
1 small onion
2 medium courgettes
1 litre/1³/₄ pints water
4 ripe tomatoes

For the marinade
150 ml/5 fl oz olive oil
3 tablespoons balsamic vinegar
50 ml/2 fl oz water
2–3 fine slivers of peeled garlic
12 basil leaves
2 sprigs of thyme

Preheat the oven to 200°C/400°F/gas mark 6.

Cut the stem off the aubergine and discard it. Slice the aubergine into 1 cm/¹/₂ in slices and sprinkle with 1 teaspoon salt. Leave to degorge for about 30 minutes, then rinse and pat dry.

In a large roasting tin heat 6 tablespoons of the olive oil and sear the aubergine slices on both sides, colouring them slightly. Roast in the oven for 8 minutes, 4 minutes on each side. Remove from the oven, drain on absorbent paper, and reserve.

Turn up the oven temperature to 230°C/450°F/gas mark 8.

Make a few slits lengthways down each of the peppers, brush with 1 tablespoon of the olive oil, and place on a roasting tray lined with kitchen foil. Roast in the oven for 20 minutes until the skin has blistered. Remove from the oven, peel, cut each pepper in half and remove the stem and seeds. Slice each half in two. Reserve.

Peel the onion and cut it into four 5 mm/¹/₄ in rings. Pan-fry in the remaining olive oil over a medium heat, covered. Turn after 5 minutes with a fish slice so as not to break up the rings and cook for a further 5–6 minutes, colouring them lightly. Season with salt and pepper.

Slice the courgettes into 5 mm/¹/₄ in thick slices on a slight diagonal. Bring the water plus 1 tablespoon salt to the boil, and boil the courgettes for a maximum of 1 minute. Drain, reserving the cooking water. Refresh the courgettes under cold running water to keep their colour. Pat dry and reserve.

Remove the stalks from the tomatoes and plunge them for 3–5 seconds into the boiling water reserved from cooking the courgettes. Lift out of the water, refresh under cold running water, then drain and skin. Slice the flesh into quarters and remove the seeds. Reserve.

Mix the oil for the marinade with the vinegar and water, and season with salt and pepper. Lay the slices of aubergine, peppers, onions, courgettes and tomatoes in a single layer in a large dish. Sprinkle the marinade mixture over them, then add the garlic, basil and thyme, and freshly ground pepper. Cover with clingfilm and leave to marinate for at least 6 hours.

Serve straight from the marinating dish, or arrange the vegetables on individual plates.

Chef's Notes

If the aubergine is over-ripe, it will be hollow and full of seeds. During the marinating time the slices will also lose their colour. Always choose aubergines that are heavy and firm and which do not sound hollow when tapped.

The olive oil used should be the very best quality, first-pressing (virgin) oil.

The salting of the aubergines is done for two reasons: it removes some of the excessive bitterness, and also draws out some of the water.

Variations

Anchovies, black olives in olive oil, marinated sardines, fennel, pan-fried little fillets of red mullet, or slivers of Parmesan cheese should be added as well.

A tomato vinaigrette could be served separately.

Deep-fried tarragon or basil could also be added to give a festive look.

Recipe reproduced from Raymond Blanc's
Cooking for Friends, *published by Headline*

Smoked Mackerel Pâté

SERVES 4–6

4 smoked mackerel fillets, skinned and flaked
225 g/8 oz low fat cream cheese
2 tablespoons low fat crème fraîche
1 tablespoon chopped chives
finely grated zest and juice of 1 lemon
salt and freshly ground black pepper

*P*lace the mackerel fillets in a shallow bowl or food processor. Add the cream cheese, crème fraîche and chives and beat until smooth. Add the lemon zest and juice and season to taste with salt and pepper.

Pack into 4–6 individual ramekins or one large dish. Cover with clingfilm and chill in the refrigerator until ready to serve.

ELAINE SACKS

Spinach Spread

300 g/10 oz frozen chopped spinach, defrosted and squeezed dry
175 g/6 oz mayonnaise
$^1/_2$ cup chopped spring onions
$^1/_2$ cup chopped dill
juice of 1 lemon
salt

*M*ix everything together. Pack into a dish, chill and serve with wholemeal toast.

> Oak Lodge School has a particularly warm place in my heart because we watched it being built! We lived right across the road until 1979, and saw the children coming and going every day. I hear only the highest praise for all the wonderful work you are doing now with children who have learning difficulties, and I am proud to be associated with your work.
>
> *Elaine Sacks*

Pineapple Madras Salad

Serves 4

Poach the pineapple slices with the curry powder in the pineapple juice for 2 minutes. Leave to cool.

Drain and cut the pineapple into mouth-sized bites, reserving the juice. Mix together with the cucumber, sultanas, tomato and celery. Chill well until required.

Divide between four plates and garnish with some salad leaves.

Mix a couple of tablespoons of the curried pineapple juice with the yogurt. Drizzle over the salad and serve.

4 slices fresh pineapple
$^1/_2$ teaspoon hot curry powder
150 ml ($^1/_4$ pt) natural pineapple juice
50 g (2 oz) cucumber, diced
25 g (1 oz) sultanas
1 large tomato, diced
1 stick celeery, chopped
150 ml ($^1/_4$ pt) natural low fat yogurt
salad leaves to garnish

Aubergine and Chick Peas

1/4 cup olive oil

1 large onion, chopped

1 green pepper, seeded and cut
  in strips

1 medium aubergine, cut into
  1/2 inch cubes

1 tsp salt

pepper

dried oregano

19 oz can of tomatoes

2 cups canned chick peas

1/4 cup chopped parsley

Heat half the oil in a heavy skillet over medium heat. Add onion, green pepper and aubergine and stir for about 5 minutes.

Add the remaining ingredients, except the parsley, and toss lightly. Cover and cook over very low heat for about 30 minutes. Serve sprinkled with parsley.

Served cold this dish can be a starter or a relish with cold roast. Served hot it makes a fine part of any main course.

Soups & Starters

Pasta

Spaghetti Dolce

SERVES 4

*C*ook the spaghetti in a saucepan of boiling water for about 8 minutes or until *al dente*.

Meanwhile, mix together the cream, brandy and sugar to taste. When the spaghetti is ready, drain and immediately pour over the cream mixture. Toss well and serve at once.

I do wish you every success with your book.

450 g/1 lb spaghetti
150 ml/5 fl oz double cream
2 tablespoons brandy
caster sugar

HARTLEY BOOTH MP

I am delighted that Oak Lodge School are compiling a recipe book and I am very happy to send this message of goodwill to the school.

As there is only one thing that I cook there is one recipe that I can give you. This is my own variety of Spaghetti Napolitan! I attach the recipe!

Extra Special Spaghetti Neapolitan

Cook the spaghetti in plenty of boiling water until *al dente*.

Meanwhile, fry the onion in a little of the oil until soft. Heat the tomato purée and tomatoes together with the remaining oil, herbs and salt and pepper to taste. Mix the onions and tomato sauce before the onions brown.

Serve with a huge bowl of grated Parmesan or hard, mature Cheddar cheese and a large bottle of Chianti or Vieto wine.

450 g/1 lb spaghetti
8 tablespoons olive oil
1 huge onion, finely chopped
2 small cans of best tomato
    purée
1 x 400 g/14 oz can of Italian
    tomatoes, drained and
    chopped
mixed fresh herbs, such as
    basil, rosemary, tarragon,
    chopped nasturtium
salt and freshly ground black
    pepper

Pasta

Spaghetti Carbonara

SERVES 4

1 tablespoon butter
2 tablespoons olive oil
2 garlic cloves, crushed
8 rashers of smoked bacon, cut
    into 2.5 cm/1 in pieces
¼ wine glass dry white wine
4 tablespoons single cream
1 egg (optional)
100 g/4 oz freshly grated
    Parmesan cheese (optional)

Cook the spaghetti in plenty of boiling water for about 7 minutes until *al dente*. My children like to throw a piece at the kitchen wall – if it sticks, it's cooked!

Meanwhile, heat the butter and oil in a frying pan. Add the garlic and bacon and fry until crisp and brown.

Remove the pan from the heat. Add the wine and stir well. Allow to sizzle to burn off some of the liquid. (Be careful not to do this over the heat or the contents of the pan may burst into flames.)

Warm a serving dish in a moderate oven. Add the cream and the egg and cheese if used. Mix well.

Drain the spaghetti, add to the dish and toss well. Place the bacon and pan juices on top and toss again. Serve immediately with a crisp green salad.

ED STUART

Spaghetti with Garlic and Oil

SERVES 4

450 g/1 lb spaghetti
9 tablespoons olive oil
2 garlic cloves, chopped
salt and freshly ground black
    pepper
2 tablespoons chopped parsley

Cook the spaghetti in plenty of boiling water until *al dente*.
Meanwhile, put 6 tablespoons of the oil, the garlic and salt into a saucepan. Sauté the garlic over a low heat until golden.

Drain the spaghetti and transfer to a warm bowl. Add the oil and garlic sauce. Toss well, adding pepper and parsley. Mix in the remaining oil and serve immediately.

Pasta for a Summer's Day

SERVES 4

$\mathcal{Y}$ou must use a lot of water to cook pasta. I would never cook spaghetti for 4 in less than 12 pints of water with a tablespoon of salt. For the penne 8 pints would probably be enough.

Don't overcook the pasta; it should be *al dente*, that is, slightly firm at the centre. Start tasting pieces after 5 minutes' boiling – every brand has a different cooking time and cooking times also seem to vary in different parts of Italy. In any case, never go by what it says on the packet. For those of you who may be unfamiliar with cooking spaghetti, take care when you drain the pasta into a colander that it doesn't slide out backwards into the sink.

What you're really making here is a salad. Chop the parsley and if you have the energy tear up the basil. Warm the olive oil in a small saucepan. Spear the garlic clove on a fork and wipe it round the saucepan containing the oil. When you are aware of the smell of the garlic coming from the pan, throw the garlic away (this is a delicately flavoured dish; there is no point in having parsley and basil if the whole dish is going to be overwhelmed by the flavour of garlic).

When the pasta is drained, put it into a large serving bowl and pour over the flavoured oil and lemon juice. Mix well and season with pepper. Mix again. Serve in individual bowls sprinkled with the parsley and basil.

500 g/20 oz spaghetti or penne (ideally non-ribbed penne lisce)
50 g/2 oz parsley
16 fresh basil leaves
4 tablespoons good Italian olive oil
1 garlic clove
juice of $^1/_2$ lemon
salt and freshly ground black pepper

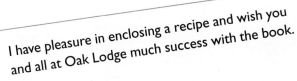

I have pleasure in enclosing a recipe and wish you and all at Oak Lodge much success with the book.

Yours sincerely,

Tom Conti

Penne with Cauliflower and Chilli

SERVES 4

1 large cauliflower
3 garlic cloves
2 tablespoons tomato purée
1 teaspoon harissa paste
3 tablespoons extra virgin olive
   oil
450 g/1 lb tomatoes, skinned,
   deseeded and chopped
salt and freshly ground black
   pepper
225 g/8 oz penne

Cut the cauliflower into 1cm/½ in florets. Finely chop the garlic cloves. Dilute the tomato purée with 3 tablespoons water and stir in the harissa. Heat the oil in a deep frying pan or sauté pan. Cook the garlic until it gives off an aroma, then add the tomato solution and the chopped tomato. Season with salt and pepper. Simmer the sauce for a couple of minutes. Add the cauliflower and cook, covered, for 7 minutes, stirring occasionally. It should remain on the firm side.

Meanwhile, cook the pasta in plenty of boiling water until *al dente*. Drain it, though not too dry, and toss it with the cauliflower. Adjust the seasoning and serve.

Recipe reprinted from
Evergreen: Classic Vegetarian Cookery
published by Bantam Books

Best wishes
Annie Bell

Pasta con Sarde

SERVES 3–4

5 tablespoons olive oil
½ small onion, finely chopped
2 medium garlic cloves
   (optional), finely chopped
1 x 45 g/1¾ oz can of anchovy
   fillets
1 x 225 g/8 oz can of tomatoes
25 g/1 oz sultanas
25 g/1 oz pine nuts
2 x 120 g/4½ oz cans of
   sardines in oil, drained
salt and freshly ground black
   pepper
350 g/12 oz penne or other
   tubular pasta
2 tablespoons fennel seeds,
   crushed

In Sicily most of the ingredients would be fresh, but this is a very good stand-by dish using ingredients from the store cupboard.

Heat the oil in a large frying pan and sauté the onion, garlic if used, and anchovies until softened. Add the tomatoes and sultanas and cook for 10 minutes. Add the pine nuts and sardines, simmer gently for a further 5 minutes, then season to taste with salt and pepper.

Meanwhile, cook the pasta in plenty of boiling water until *al dente* (not too soft). Drain and add to the sauce. Stir together, add the fennel and serve immediately, with a green salad.

Pasta

Pasta Primavera

SERVES 4

*O*nce spurned by dieters, there has been a rethink on pasta and it is now recognized as an excellent source of complex carbohydrates and one of the perfect energy foods. Choose wholewheat pasta as it contains fibre, and serve it with a light tomato and herb sauce: do not be tempted into topping it with a rich or creamy sauce high in calories. This scrumptious, healthy dish will be savoured by children.

Here is one of my favourite recipes for pasta.

Cook the pasta in plenty of boiling water for about 12 minutes or until *al dente*. Drain and refresh with boiling water to remove excess starch. Break the broccoli head into florets and cook in a steamer or colander over boiling water for about 7 minutes or until cooked, but still crunchy.

Sauté the onions in a little butter until soft. (If you have a microwave no butter is needed. Put the onions into a bowl with about 1 cm/$\frac{1}{2}$ in water in the bottom. Cover with clingfilm and cook on High for $2\frac{1}{2}$ minutes.) When cooked, drain and add to the broccoli.

Cook the courgettes in the steamer for about 5 minutes, or boil in water until cooked but still firm.

Clean the mushrooms with a little salt and absorbent paper, or peel them. Place under a hot grill for a few minutes. Drain on absorbent paper. When cooked, cut into large chunks.

Place the tomatoes in boiling water for 10 seconds, then transfer them immediately to cold water. Remove the skins, quarter, and cut each quarter in half again. Remove the seeds.

Combine all the vegetables except the broccoli and add the garlic. Season with salt and pepper. Add the vegetables to the pasta and reheat gently in a saucepan.

Return the broccoli to the steamer for 1 minute to reheat, then carefully add to the hot pasta and vegetables. This prevents the broccoli from breaking up.

Add a little grated Parmesan if liked, but this is not essential. Serve warm, not too hot.

450 g/1 lb penne
1 head of broccoli
2 medium onions, roughly chopped
2 medium courgettes, cut into 5 cm/2 in strips
8 large mushrooms
2 large tomatoes
2 garlic cloves, crushed
grated Parmesan cheese (optional)

Copyright © Jemstar International

Pasta

Grilled Sea Bass with Fettucine and Ratatouille Sauce

SERVES 4

450 g/1 lb pasta dough (or bought fresh or dried fettucine)

50 g/2 oz unsalted butter

salt and freshly ground black pepper

4 sea bass fillets, each about 175–225 g/6–8oz

25 ml/1 fl oz olive oil

For the ratatouille

1 red pepper, deseeded

1 green pepper, deseeded

2 shallots

1/2 aubergine

1 courgette

25 g/1 oz unsalted butter

25 g/1 fl oz olive oil

For the red pepper coulis

1 large red pepper, deseeded and sliced

2 teaspoons oil

Make the fettucine: roll the dough through a pasta machine several times until about 1 mm/$^1/_{16}$ in thick, then pass through the noodle cutter and leave to rest. If you do not have a pasta machine, the dough can be divided, rolled several times until very thin, then cut by hand into ribbons; a pizza wheel is the easiest way to cut the pasta.

Preheat the grill to medium. Grease a baking tray with some of the butter.

Make the ratatouille: cut the vegetables into 5 mm/$^1/_4$ in dice. Melt the butter with the olive oil in a large pan. Add the diced vegetables and cook for about 3–4 minutes or until just softened.

Make the red pepper coulis: simmer the red pepper until tender, then peel and liquidize with the oil.

In a separate pan, warm the red pepper coulis, then add the vegetables. Season to taste with salt and pepper.

Lay the sea bass fillets skin side up on the prepared baking tray and grill for about 8 minutes, turning once.

Meanwhile, bring a large pan of water to the boil with the olive oil and a pinch of salt added. When boiling, drop in the pasta and move it around with a fork. If it is fresh, it will only take a few minutes to cook. For dried pasta, follow the instructions on the packet. Drain through a colander, season with salt and pepper and toss with the remaining butter.

Warm the ratatouille sauce and spoon onto hot plates. Sit the fettucine in the middle and lay the grilled sea bass on top. Serve immediately.

Pasta with Pork and Basil

SERVES 4

Brush the pork steaks with egg and season with the Parmesan, basil and garlic (if used), as well as salt and pepper.

Fry the steaks in butter in a frying pan until cooked right through. Transfer to a casserole. Sauté the mushrooms and add to the pork steaks.

Make the sauce: deglaze the frying pan with the chicken stock. Make a smooth rich sauce with the butter, flour, stock and cream. Add any juices that have collected in the casserole and simmer for 4 minutes.

Remove from the heat and season with salt and pepper. Stir in the Parmesan and mustard.

Pour the sauce over the pork steaks, cover and keep hot in a low oven.

Cook the pasta in plenty of boiling water until *al dente* and drain well. Add to the casserole together with the herbs. Toss gently to mix well. Serve immediately.

4 pork steaks
1 egg, beaten
1 tablespoon freshly grated
    Parmesan cheese
2 tablespoons chopped basil
1 garlic clove, crushed
salt and freshly ground black
    pepper
a little butter for frying
175 g/6 oz mushrooms, thickly
    sliced
225 g/8 oz fusilli or other fresh
    pasta shapes
a handful of chopped basil,
    chives and parsley

For the sauce
15 g/½ oz butter
1½ tablespoons plain flour
150 ml/5 fl oz double cream
290 ml/scant ½ pint chicken
    stock
2 tablespoons freshly grated
    Parmesan cheese
2 teaspoons Dijon mustard

Salsa Michele

(A quick and delicious version of Salsa Amatriciana)

SERVES 3–4

450 g/1 lb tagliatelle, fettucine or linguine (fresh, if possible)

2 tablespoons extra virgin olive oil

1 large onion, chopped

2 x 400 g/14 oz cans of tomatoes, coarsely chopped

6–8 garlic cloves, minced or crushed

225 g/8 oz Parma ham, roughly chopped

2 tablespoons chopped fresh oregano

3 tablespoons torn fresh basil leaves

175 ml/6 fl oz dry white wine, such as Pinot Grigio

a pinch of salt

$1/2$ teaspoon (or to taste) red pepper flakes, or 1–2 dried hot red peppers (use judiciously – you can guess what will happen!)

50 g/2 oz freshly grated Parmesan cheese (optional)

Cook the pasta in plenty of water. Drain. Toss with 1 teaspoon of the oil. Set aside.

Pour the remaining oil into a large frying pan and briefly sauté the onion over a medium heat until soft. Add the tomatoes with their juice, garlic, ham and wine. Stir occasionally, and cook gently for about 5 minutes until some of the liquid is absorbed (resist the urge to consume the sauce completely at this point).

Add the fresh herbs, the sugar and the red pepper flakes (if you use the dried peppers do not forget to remove them before serving!). You will not need salt; the Parma ham imparts enough salty flavour to the sauce.

Cook gently for a further 5 minutes to reduce the sauce. Taste and adjust seasonings if necessary.

Serve over the fresh pasta and sprinkle with freshly grated cheese if used.

Buon Gusto!

Fish & Shellfish

Julie Walters

Dear Caroline Esdaile ~
My recipe is :- 2 pieces of whole
meal bread (buttered) ½ pt fresh
cockles, spread those on bread, sprinkle
with freshly ground pepper cover with
other piece of bread + eat!
All the best to everyone at
Oak Lodge School + good luck with
the book ~ Sincerely, Julie Walters

SIR ROBIN DAY

Kedgeree

One of my favourite dishes is kedgeree. I can't give you a
detailed recipe, but the ingredients are:

haddock
rice
butter
onions
garlic

hardboiled eggs
red and green peppers
salt
pepper
fresh ginger, grated

I'm afraid I can't give you the cooking details.

Fish & Shellfish

Roast Sea Scallops with Sauce Vierge

SERVES 4

8 large fresh scallops
salt and freshly ground white
   pepper
4 teaspoons olive oil

To serve
1 quantity Sauce Vierge
fresh herbs, such as tarragon,
   chives, chervil

*W*ash the scallops quickly in cold water, pat dry and refrigerate for at least 30 minutes. When the scallops are firm, slice each in half. Season with a little salt.

   Heat the olive oil in a frying pan. Sauté the scallop slices in the hot oil for about 2 minutes, turning them as each side becomes golden-brown. Do not overcook – the scallops should be medium rare.

   Pour 2 tablespoons of the sauce on to each plate, and arrange the scallop slices on top. Garnish with herbs.

Sauce Vierge

SERVES 4

85 ml/3 fl oz olive oil
25 ml/1 fl oz lemon juice
1 teaspoon crushed coriander
   seeds
8 basil leaves, cut into julienne
   strips
2 tomatoes, skinned, deseeded
   and diced

*H*eat the oil gently in a small pan, then add the lemon juice. Remove from the heat. Add the coriander and basil, and leave to infuse in the warm oil for a few minutes. Add the tomato dice and serve immediately.

Recipe reprinted from Wild Food from Land and Sea,
published by Ebury Press

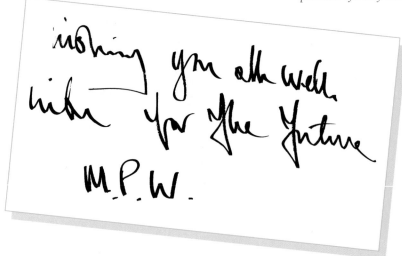

Fish & Shellfish

Spinach, Scallops and Bacon

SERVES 4

*C*ut the white scallop meat into discs and season well with salt and pepper. Leave to rest for 30 minutes. The difference in taste between shellfish that has been pre-salted and shellfish that has not is amazing.

Meanwhile, cook the spinach and drain well, pressing it down in a colander to remove excess water. Portion out the spinach among 4 serving plates and keep warm.

In a frying pan, sauté the bacon until crisp. Top the spinach with the drained bacon.

Clean the pan, add the butter or oil and quickly sauté the scallop discs. Don't overcook: they need only a few seconds to brown the edges.

Add the drained scallop discs to the bacon-topped spinach. Pour a few slurps of sherry vinegar into the pan, heat until bubbling and pour over the dish. Serve immediately.

Yum, yum.

You can also use uncooked young spinach leaves with the stalks removed instead of cooked spinach for a lighter, more summery dish.

8 scallops
450 g/1 lb fresh or frozen
    spinach
salt and freshly ground black
    pepper
diced bacon (same weight as
    scallops)

Tiger Prawns in Filo with Mango Sauce

SERVES 4

16 raw tiger prawns
sea salt and freshly ground black
 pepper
16 x 10 cm/4 in squares of filo
 pastry dough
unsalted butter, melted
32 large fresh basil leaves
1 egg yolk
vegetable oil for deep-frying
4 handfuls of mixed salad leaves
4 tablespoons soy dressing

For the mango sauce
1 large ripe mango
1 hardboiled egg yolk
4 tablespoons mayonnaise
2 teaspoons finely shredded
 fresh basil
salt and freshly ground white
 pepper

Make the mango sauce: peel the mango, then cut the flesh from the flat central stone. Chop the flesh coarsely: you should have about 100g/4oz.

Put the flesh into a food processor or blender with the hardboiled egg yolk and mayonnaise and work until smooth.

Press the mixture through a fine sieve into a bowl. Stir in the basil and season to taste with salt and pepper. Set the sauce aside.

Peel the prawns, then make a shallow cut down the rounded back of each and remove the dark intestinal vein. Rinse the prawns and pat dry with absorbent paper. Season with salt and pepper.

Put a filo square on the work surface and brush it with melted butter. Set a basil leaf in the centre and put a prawn on top. Lightly beat the egg yolk and brush a little on the edges of the filo square.

Fold 2 opposite sides of the square over the prawn and press to seal. Press the ends together to seal. Wrap and seal the remaining prawns in the same way.

Heat oil in a deep-fryer to 165–175°C.

Meanwhile, wash and dry the salad leaves thoroughly.

When the oil is hot, add the prawns in filo, 4 at a time. Fry for 3 minutes or until golden and crisp, turning them over a few times so that they brown evenly. Drain on absorbent paper.

At the end of frying, turn up the heat under the pan until the oil is 180°C. Add the remaining basil leaves and fry for a few seconds until crisp, bright green and translucent; drain.

Toss the salad leaves in the soy dressing, then divide among the plates, piling the leaves in a mound.

Arrange the prawns in filo in the centre of the salad and garnish with the fried basil. Serve with the mango sauce.

Soy Dressing

100 ml/3^1/$_2$ fl oz orange juice
1 tablespoon white wine vinegar
1 tablespoon soy sauce
4 tablespoons olive oil
freshly ground black pepper

Put the orange juice into a small pan and boil until reduced to 1 tablespoon. Set aside to cool completely. Combine all the remaining ingredients in a bowl, add the concentrated orange juice and whisk well to mix.

Fish & Shellfish

Oysters with Herb Garlic Butter

SERVES 4

In a small bowl, combine butter, garlic and parsley and mix to a smooth paste. Set aside. In a medium bowl, combine the lime juice and the brandy. Shuck the oysters and place in the lime/brandy mixture. Discard the top shell and rinse the bottom shell of all sand and debris.

In each shell, layer the following ingredients in order: 1 teaspoon herb butter, one drained oyster, $\frac{1}{2}$ oz cooked lobster or crabmeat, a bit of diced tomato, 1 teaspoon ketchup and 1 teaspoon caviare. Flatten the mound slightly with the back of a spoon and sprinkle with half a tablespoon of Parmesan.

Place the oysters on a bed of rock salt in a boiler pan. Boil for 3–4 minutes.

5 tablespoons plus 1 teaspoon butter, softened
1 tablespoon finely chopped parsley
2 garlic cloves, minced
juice of 2 limes
4 tablespoons brandy
16 fresh oysters, preferably Belon
8 oz cooked lobster or crabmeat
2 medium tomatoes, skinned, deseeded and diced
5 tablespoons plus 1 teaspoon tomato ketchup
5 tablespoons plus 1 teaspoon caviare
6 tablespoons freshly grated Parmesan cheese
rock salt

Steamed Fish Fingers

SERVES 4

100 g/4 oz monkfish
100 g/4 oz salmon
100 g/4 oz swordfish
100 g/4 oz fresh tuna
2 tablespoons chopped parsley
125 ml/4 fl oz soy sauce
125 ml/4 fl oz water
1 tablespoon grated fresh ginger
1 tablespoon rice wine vinegar
grated zest and juice
　of 1 orange

*C*ut each piece of fish into 4 'fingers' and place in a steamer. Set the steamer above water in the bottom of a pan with a tight-fitting lid. Steam for about 4 minutes.

Meanwhile, make the sauce. In a small saucepan, combine the parsley, soy sauce, water, ginger, vinegar, orange zest and juice. Heat gently.

Place the fish fingers in a tent shape in the centre of a dish and pour the sauce on top. Serve immediately. This dish is especially nice when served on a bed of steamed kale or on a nest of spinach pasta.

Fish & Shellfish

Spicy Prawns with Couscous Salad

SERVES 4

*M*elt the butter in a pan and add the saffron liquid with the chicken or vegetable stock. Bring to the boil, then stir in the couscous. Cover and remove the pan from the heat. Set aside for about 8 minutes until the liquid is absorbed. Transfer to a bowl and fluff up grains with a fork.

Add the celery, raisins, spring onions, parsley, coriander and pine kernels. Mix gently and leave to stand, uncovered.

In a bowl, mix together the lemon juice, cinnamon and seasoning. Whisk in 100ml/3½fl oz of the oil until blended. Pour over the couscous, toss and check the seasoning.

Shell the prawns, split in half lengthwise and de-vein. Season with salt and pepper. Heat the remaining oil in a frying pan and sauté the prawns for about 2 minutes. Stir in the black bean paste and cook for a few further seconds.

Arrange prawns over couscous and garnish with coriander sprigs.

40 g/1½ oz butter

20 g/¾ oz saffron threads, infused in 2 tablespoons warm stock

350 ml/12 fl oz vegetable or chicken stock

250 g/9 oz couscous

100 g/4oz celery, thinly sliced

75 g/3 oz seedless raisins, softened in warm water and drained

1 bunch spring onions, thinly sliced

15 g/½ oz each chopped fresh parsley and coriander

50–75 g/2–3 oz pine kernels

juice of 2 lemons

a pinch of ground cinnamon

100 ml/3½ fl oz olive oil, plus 1 tablespoon

8 large prawns

1 tablespoon black bean paste

salt and freshly ground black pepper

coriander sprigs, to garnish

Fish & Shellfish

Grilled Sea Bass with Fennel

SERVES 8

1 sea bass, about
    1.75–2.25 g/4–5 lb
3 heads of fennel
2 onions, thinly sliced
125 ml/4 fl oz olive oil, plus
    extra for brushing
dried fennel stalks
pared zest and juice of 1 lemon
salt and freshly ground black
    pepper

Trim, clean and gut the sea bass through the gills. Rinse well, pat dry and set aside.

Remove the feathery tops of the fennel, chop them finely and reserve. Halve the fennel bulbs lengthways, discard hard cores and slice thinly.

Gently cook the onion and fennel in two tablespoons of the oil until just tender. Add the reserved chopped fennel fronds and salt and pepper. Cool. Spoon the stuffing into the fish through the mouth.

Place the fish in a shallow dish with the dried fennel stalks, lemon zest and juice and the remaining oil. Cover and leave to marinate for 2–3 hours.

Remove the fish from the marinade and place in a grill pan or on a wire rack above the grid of a barbecue. Brush all over with oil, then grill for 10 minutes. Turn over and grill for a further 10 minutes. Turn once again and grill for 10 minutes more. Check that the fish is cooked; it should feel tender, offering little resistance to the touch. If not, continue to grill for a few minutes more, taking care not to overcook.

Just before serving, remove fennel stalks from the marinade and place them over the barbecue to bring out their flavour. Arrange on a platter with the fish on top.

Fish & Shellfish

Monkfish Teriyaki

SERVES 4

Peel the mooli and, using a mandolin or sharp knife, finely slice lengthwise. Layer a few lengths at a time on top of each other and cut into very fine noodle-like strips. Soak in iced water for about 30 minutes, drain and reserve.

Lightly season the fish with salt and pepper, and leave for 15 minutes to firm up slightly.

Make the teriyaki marinade by mixing together the mirin, sake and soy sauce in a shallow dish. Add the fish steaks, turn to coat evenly, cover and leave to marinate for about 1 hour in a cool place.

Remove the fish from the marinade and pat dry. Grill or fry in the oil initially over a medium heat, but quickly reducing temperature. Cook for 4–5 minutes until golden brown. Turn fish over and brush with some marinade. Cook for a further 4–5 minutes, brushing occasionally with the remaining marinade.

Meanwhile, lightly brush the leeks with oil and grill or fry until golden brown. Serve the fish steaks with the cold mooli noodles and warm baby leeks.

Recipe taken from BBC-TV's Good Top Chef

1 mooli (white radish)
4 monkfish steaks with bones, about 250 g/9 oz each
150 ml/5 fl oz mirin
125 ml/4 fl oz sake
85 ml/3 fl oz dark soy sauce
a little olive oil, plus extra for brushing
9 baby leeks, trimmed and cut into 5 cm/2 in lengths
salt and freshly ground black pepper

Happy Cooking!

Fiskekaker

(Norwegian Fish Cakes)

SERVES 4

450 g/1 lb fresh haddock, skinned and boned

110 ml/4 fl oz full cream milk

1 tablespoon cornflour

1¹/₂ tablespoons chopped parsley (not traditional but I like it!)

110 ml/4 fl oz crème fraîche, or soured cream mixed with double cream

salt and freshly ground white pepper

butter and oil for frying

Cut the haddock up roughly and process with just enough of the milk to make a smooth mixture. Sprinkle over the cornflour and parsley and add the crème fraîche, salt and pepper. Process again, gradually adding more of the milk until you have a fluffy, light but still firm mixture.

Shape tablespoons of the mixture into small flat, round cakes, about 1cm/¹/₂in thick. Fry in butter or butter and oil until browned. Serve with shrimp sauce.

Rekesaus

(Norwegian Shrimp Sauce)

SERVES 4–6

450 g/1 lb cooked shrimps or small prawns in their shells

300 ml/10 fl oz fish stock

25 g/1 oz butter

25 g/1 oz plain flour

150 ml/5 fl oz double cream

1 lemon

1 tablespoon finely chopped fresh dill

salt and freshly ground white pepper

Shell the shrimps or prawns. Chop the shells and heads roughly in a food processor and put into a saucepan with the fish stock. Bring to the boil, then simmer for 10 minutes. Strain and reserve the stock. Chop the shrimps or prawns roughly.

Melt the butter in a saucepan and stir in the flour. Stir over a low heat for 1 minute, then draw off the heat. Gradually mix in the stock, a little at a time, to make a smooth, smooth sauce. Then stir in the cream. Bring back to the boil, then simmer for 5 minutes or so. Add a generous squeeze of lemon juice and the dill and season to taste with salt and pepper.

Fish & Shellfish

Cullen Skink

SERVES 4

Skin the haddock, put into a pan and cover with boiling water. Simmer for about 5 minutes or until the fish is cooked.

Remove the bones, return them to the stock and simmer for about 30 minutes.

Meanwhile, flake the fish into a separate pan. Strain the cooking liquid and add to the flaked fish and milk. Bring to the boil, then add enough mashed potatoes to make a creamy consistency. Season to taste with salt and pepper. Add the butter and serve hot.

I Finnan haddock
575 ml/I pint milk
mashed potatoes
a small piece of butter
salt and freshly ground black
   pepper

MIRIAM MARGOLYES

Grilled Plaice

Like most Jewish mothers, mine could fry fish wonderfully, but like some Jewish children I got fat, and can't eat fried stuff any more. So my recipe is for Grilled Plaice. It's so simple and so quick and so delicious – I have it for any meal at any time.

Wash the plaice and pat dry.

Cut all the vegetables into small pieces or slices. Place them in a grill pan with the plaice. Add a knob of butter or some oil and grill for 6–8 minutes, basting now and again. The less butter used, the less fattening. Season to taste with salt and pepper and serve. It never fails.

plaice – on or off the bone (on
   is sweeter)
spring onions
tomatoes
mushrooms
butter or olive oil
salt and freshly ground black
   pepper

Miriam Margolyes

Fish & Shellfish

Poached Salmon

6 black peppercorns
2–3 bay leaves
1 teaspoon white wine vinegar
juice of $1/_2$ lemon
4 salmon steaks or a piece of
   salmon tail
cucumber and lemon slices, to
   garnish
mayonnaise, to serve

Fill a saucepan two-thirds full of water and add the peppercorns, bay leaves, vinegar, and lemon juice.

Cover and bring to the boil. Add the salmon, cover again and immediately turn off the heat. Leave for 1 hour before serving hot, or several hours to serve cold.

Serve garnished with cucumber and lemon accompanied with mayonnaise.

This comes with our best wishes for the important and caring work of you and your staff in caring for some of the most vulnerable young people in our society

ARSENAL FOOTBALL CLUB

Dover Sole

8 Dover soles
seasoned flour
150g/6oz melted butter
parsley, butter and lemon slices
   to garnish

This is one of the team's favourite dishes for the night before a match. We serve it with chips, boiled potatoes and two vegetables. For a first course the lads have a choice of soup or spaghetti bolognese, and for pudding ice cream, fruit salad, rice pudding or bananas.

Clean and gut the soles and remove the skin from the upper dark side. Wash and dry thoroughly. Coat in seasoned flour and brush with melted butter. Grill under moderate heat for 6–10 minutes depending on size, turning once and basting with butter. Serve garnished with butter, lemon and parsley.

Fish & Shellfish

Fish Pie

SERVES 6–8

You may use any firm white fish mix for this. Cod and salmon is a lovely combination. Or why not try hoki? Enjoy!

Preheat the oven to 190°C/375°F/gas mark 5.

Gently poach the smoked and fresh cod in the milk in a large saucepan for about 5 minutes. Remove the fish and reserve the milk.

Soften the leeks in a little of the butter until transparent but not browned. Flake the fish into a shallow dish, removing skin and bones, top with the leeks and hardboiled eggs.

Return the cooled milk, cream, remaining butter and flour to the pan, set over a low heat and using a little hand whisk, whisk until the sauce thickens. Add salt and pepper to taste and the parsley. Pour over the fish and allow to cool.

Top with creamy mashed potato and bake in the oven for about 40 minutes until golden-brown.

450 g/1 lb smoked cod fillets
450 g/1 lb fresh cod fillets
300 ml/10 fl oz milk
3 leeks, chopped
75 g/3 oz butter
4 hardboiled eggs, quartered
300 ml/10 fl oz single cream
75 g/3 oz plain flour
salt and freshly ground black
   pepper
900 g/2 lb creamy mashed
   potatoes

Kiri Te Kanawa

With best wishes to Oak Lodge School —
keep up your tremendously important
work.

With Compliments

Fish Dish

*A*sk the fishmonger to gut and clean the bass, which is a tricky fish to handle.

1 freshly caught sea bass, about 2.25 kg/5 lb
1 bulbs of fresh fennel, sliced
salt and freshly ground black pepper
150 ml/5 fl oz dry white wine

Preheat the oven to 180°C/350°F/gas mark 4.

Put the fennel inside the fish and season with salt and pepper inside and out.

Place on a sheet of kitchen foil and pour over the wine.

Wrap the foil loosely, making a parcel, and place on a baking tray. Bake in the oven for about 40 minutes or until cooked through.

Serve with fresh vegetables or salad, new potatoes and a crisp dry white wine.

N.B. The sea bass may also be cooked on a barbecue, still in the loose foil parcel, for 20 minutes on each side.

SIR DEREK JACOBI

Cheese and Tuna Casserole

SERVES 2

50 g/2 oz butter
1 medium onion
4 teaspoons plain flour
2 cups of milk
1/2 cup of grated mature Cheddar cheese
1 cup of cooked rice
1 x 225 g/8 oz can of tuna
fresh white breadcrumbs
salt and freshly ground black pepper

*P*reheat the oven to 180°C/350°F/gas mark 4.

Melt half the butter in a frying pan and fry the onion until soft. Add the flour and milk blended together. Boil for 2–3 minutes. Stir in the cheese, rice, tuna and salt and pepper.

Put into a greased casserole, sprinkle with breadcrumbs and dot with the remaining butter. Cook in the oven for 30 minutes.

Fish & Shellfish

Grilled Tuna with Black-eyed Beans and Coriander

SERVES 4

Soak the black-eyed beans in water overnight.

Make a marinade by combining the crushed coriander seeds, the garlic and a quarter of the chopped coriander in the lime juice and 1 tablespoon of the oil. Place the tuna steaks in a shallow dish and spoon over the marinade. Leave to marinate in a cool place for 2 hours.

Meanwhile, discard the soaking water from the black-eyed beans, rinse and cover with fresh cold water, lightly salted, in a non-stick saucepan. Simmer, covered, for 1 hour or until the beans are tender. Drain and reserve.

Heat the remaining oil in a large frying pan. Add the onion and sweat until translucent. Stir in the chopped tomato and remove from the heat. Add the black-eyed beans, vinaigrette and the remaining chopped coriander.

Remove the fish steaks and reserve the marinade. Season the steaks with salt and pepper, then grill, preferably over charcoal, for 4 minutes on each side. Brush the steaks with marinade while cooking. Warm the bean and tomato mixture. Spoon a small mound into the centre of each plate and serve with a tuna steak placed on top.

100 g/4 oz black-eyed beans
2 teaspoons coriander seeds, crushed
2 garlic cloves, chopped
1 bunch of fresh coriander, chopped
juice of 2 limes
2 tablespoons extra virgin olive oil
4 x 150 g/5 oz tuna steaks, skinned and boned
1 small onion, finely chopped
4 tablespoons chopped, deseeded tomatoes
150 ml/5 fl oz vinaigrette
sea salt and freshly ground black pepper

Champneys is delighted to support Oak Lodge School in raising funds to provide additional amenities. Good luck to all those taking part in the fundraising.

Tuna Fish Pie

SERVES 2–3

50 g/2 oz margarine

1 tablespoon plain flour

salt and freshly ground black pepper

milk

50 g/2 oz tasty Cheddar cheese, grated

1 x 225 g/8 oz can of tuna fish (with the sign that it isn't netted)

2 bunches of parsley, chopped

3 hardboiled eggs, roughly chopped

mashed potato

*P*reheat the oven to 190°C/375°F/gas mark 5.
Grease a high-sided pie dish.

Melt the margarine in a saucepan, add the flour, salt, pepper and enough milk to make a thick white paste. Add the cheese and heat just until melted.

Add the tuna, parsley and hardboiled eggs. Mix carefully so as not to mash the mixture and pour into the pie dish. Put slices of tomato on top, if used, and then top with mashed potato, spreading it out evenly and forking it up. Bake in the oven for 20–30 minutes. Serve with any vegetable.

CHAIM TOPOL

Gefilteh Fish

SERVES 12

900 g/2 lb carp, skinned, boned and minced

3 large onions, steamed for 5 minutes, then drained and chopped

3 hardboiled eggs, chopped

1 raw egg

1 teaspoon salt

1/2 teaspoon freshly ground black pepper

3 tablespoons sugar if of Russian descent or 6 tablespoons if of Polish descent

*M*ix together the carp, steamed chopped onions, hardboiled eggs, raw egg, salt and pepper. If the mixture seems too loose, add some breadcrumbs. Divide into 12 oval fish cakes about 10 × 7.5 cm/4 × 3 in and 2 cm/3/4 in thick. Layer the bottom of a wide pot with the onion slices and half of the carrots. Add salt, pepper and the sugar. Then pour over the water. Arrange a layer of 6–8 fish cakes on top and cover with the remaining carrots to prevent the next layer from sticking. Add the remaining fish cakes and pour over enough water to cover both layers.

Bring to the boil, then simmer for 2 hours over a low heat.

Allow to cool, then lift the fish cakes from the liquid. Use some of the carrot slices to garnish the fish cakes.

Discard the onions and liquidize the remaining carrots and cooking liquid. Pour into a shallow bowl.

Chill the fish cakes and the liquid in the refrigerator: the liquid will turn to jelly. Serve cold with some chopped jelly garnishing each fish cake. Bon appetit!

Fish & Shellfish

Poultry

To all the children of Oak hodge School.
May God Bless you all!
+ George Cantuar

Chicken Toscana

SERVES 4

Simmer the chicken in the water with the onion, carrot, bouquet garni and salt and pepper for about 45–50 minutes, or until tender.

Meanwhile, chop the mushrooms finely. Peel the cucumber, cut into quarters lengthwise and then into 5cm/2in pieces; blanch and drain well.

Strain the stock from the chicken into another pan and boil until reduced to 300 ml/10 fl oz. Add the mushrooms and simmer for 3 minutes.

Carve the chicken into neat joints, and arrange in the serving dish. Slake the arrowroot with a little of the stock, add to the pan and stir until boiling. Add the chives and well-drained cucumber. Spoon over the chicken and serve immediately.

1 x 1.35 kg/3 lb roasting chicken
425 ml/^{3}/$_4$ pint water
1 onion
1 carrot
1 bouquet garni
salt and freshly ground black pepper
100 g/4 oz mushrooms
1 small cucumber
2 teaspoons arrowroot
1 tablespoon chopped chives

BEN KINGSLEY

Chicken Breasts with Sage

SERVES 2

Melt the butter with the olive oil in an iron frying pan or deep frying pan.

Coat the chicken breasts in seasoned flour and fry until golden brown.

Add the chopped sage, chopped bacon or ham, wine and chicken stock. Cover, bring to the boil and simmer for 20 minutes or until chicken is tender.

Remove chicken breasts, place on a serving dish and keep warm in a low oven.

Reduce the sauce to a creamy consistency over a medium heat. Pour over chicken breasts and serve immediately with a fresh green salad and French bread or new potatoes.

1 tbsp olive oil
30 g/1 oz butter
2 boneless, skinless chicken breasts
flour
salt and pepper
fresh sage leaves
lean bacon or prosciutto ham
small glass white wine
^{1}/$_2$ cup chicken stock

Ben Kingsley

Poultry

Chicken Tropicana

SERVES 2–4

For the marinade

3 tablespoons malt vinegar

$^1/_2$ teaspoon soy sauce

2 teaspoons clear honey

a pinch of ground ginger

juice from 1 x 225 g/8 oz can of
pineapple rings

65 ml/2$^1/_2$ fl oz tomato juice

4 medium chicken joints,
skinned

15 g/$^1/_2$ oz butter

1 large carrot, cut into strips

1 x 225 g/8 oz can of pineapple
rings

2 teaspoons cornflour

salt and freshly ground black
pepper

Mix together all the ingredients for the marinade. Place the chicken joints in a dish. Pour over the marinade, cover and chill in the refrigerator for at least 4 hours. Turn the joints occasionally.

Heat the butter in a frying pan. Remove the chicken joints from the marinade and fry in the butter for about 15 minutes or until almost cooked. Add the carrot strips and pineapple rings, cut into pieces, and fry for a further 2 minutes.

Blend the marinade smoothly with the cornflour and pour over the chicken. Bring to the boil, then simmer for 5 minutes.

Serve with plain boiled rice and vegetables.

Chicken Indienne

SERVES 8

8 good-sized chicken breasts,
boned and skinned

4 small bananas, thinly sliced

24 white grapes, halved and
deseeded

4 tablespoons crushed hazelnuts

50 g/2 oz butter

225 ml/8 fl oz double cream

350 ml/12 fl oz basic curry
sauce

Remove the fillet (the underside flap) from each chicken breast, then bat out (not too vigorously) until flat. Stuff each breast with $^1/_2$ banana, 6 grape halves and $^1/_2$ tablespoon hazelnuts. Place the fillet on top and fold the ends over to make a rectangular parcel.

Preheat the oven to 190°C/375°F/gas mark 5.

Melt the butter in a shallow roasting tin. Place the breasts, rounded side up, close together in the tin. Bake in the oven for 20–25 minutes, basting frequently, until cooked through and golden-brown.

Whisk the cream into the curry sauce. Transfer the chicken to a shallow flameproof dish and pour over the sauce. Set over a gentle heat until bubbling and slightly thickened. Remove from heat and serve with rice.

Chicken Breast with Ginger Stuffing and Orange Sauce

SERVES 4

Preheat the oven to 190°C/375°F/gas mark 5. Bat out the chicken breasts between sheets of clingfilm.

Chop together the mushrooms, onions, ginger, salt and pepper in a food processor. Turn into a pan and simmer for 30 minutes, stirring frequently, until very dry.

Spread the stuffing over the chicken breasts, roll them up and place seam side down in a roasting tin.

Cover the base of the tin with water, season the breasts with salt and pepper, cover with greaseproof paper or kitchen foil and bake for 15–20 minutes or until cooked through.

Combine the orange zest and juice, sugar, vinegar and stock and bring to the boil. Thicken with the cornflour, return to the boil in a pan and then remove from the heat.

Allow to cool for 1 minute, then whisk in the crème fraîche.

Carve the chicken breasts into slices and serve with the sauce.

Per serving – 220 Calories, medium fat, low fibre

4 x 175 g/6 oz chicken breasts
100 g/4 oz mushrooms
50 g/2 oz onions, chopped
$\frac{1}{2}$ tablespoon chopped fresh ginger
salt and freshly ground black pepper
grated zest and juice of 2 oranges
1 teaspoon sugar
2 teaspoons white wine vinegar
300 ml/10 fl oz chicken stock
1 teaspoon cornflour, blended with a little stock
2 teaspoons crème fraîche

Poultry

Chicken 'A la Pope'!

1 x 1.5 kg/3½ lb cooked chicken
2 x 300 g/10 oz packets of
    frozen broccoli
4 tablespoons mayonnaise
2 x 400 g/14 oz cans of
    Campbells condensed cream
    of chicken soup
1 soup can of milk
½ teaspoon curry powder
25 ml/1 fl oz dry white wine
1 teaspoon lemon juice
75 g/3 oz Cheddar cheese
2 packets of crisps or 4 slices of
    bread, crumbled

Preheat the oven to 150°C/300°F/gas mark 2.
    Strip the chicken meat from the bones and cut into pieces. Cook the broccoli until tender, then drain.

Grease a casserole dish. Place the chicken on the bottom, with the broccoli on top. Mix together the mayonnaise, soup, milk, curry powder, wine and lemon juice. Pour over the broccoli and chicken. Cook in the oven for 20 minutes, then turn the oven temperature up to 180°C/350°F/gas mark 4.

Sprinkle the crisps or breadcrumbs over the top of the casserole, then sprinkle with the cheese. Bake for a further 20 minutes or until brown on top.

Best wishes to all at Oak Lodge School

Cliff Richard

RABBI HUGO GRYN

Chicken Paprika and Noodles

SERVES 4–6

Fry onions until soft. Add paprika and stir gently, being careful not to allow paprika to burn. Remove onions.

Brown dried chicken pieces and combine with onions. Add tinned tomatoes, seasoning and a little boiling water. Simmer for 1–1½ hours. Add tomato puree.

1 roasting chicken, jointed
450 g/1 lb onions, finely sliced
2 tablespoons tomato puree
400 g/14 oz tin tomatoes
oil
salt, pepper and paprika

DR RUTH WESTHEIMER

Chicken with Mushrooms in Sherry

SERVES 4

Cut the chicken into bite-size pieces. Season the flour with salt and pepper.

Heat half the oil in a frying pan. Add the chicken and sauté until it starts to brown.

Heat the remaining oil in a separate frying pan and sauté the onion until translucent.

Add the mushrooms and stir-fry until softened. Set aside.

Remove the chicken from the pan. Add the sherry and stock to the pan, scrape the sediment and thicken with a little flour.

Add the chicken and mushrooms to the pan and simmer for 5 minutes.

Serve over rice.

3 whole chicken breasts, skinned and boned
flour for dredging
salt and freshly ground black pepper
6 tablespoons olive oil
1 medium onion, chopped
450 g/1 lb mushrooms, sliced
225 ml/8 fl oz medium dry sherry
225 ml/8 fl oz chicken stock

Best wishes!
Dr. Ruth
Westheimer

June 30, 1994

Poultry

Glazed Cashew Nut Chicken

SERVES 4

450 g/1 lb skinless chicken
  breast fillet
1 tablespoon oil
1 red pepper, deseeded
3 garlic cloves, crushed
2 tablespoons each fish sauce,
  oyster sauce, light brown
  sugar
75 g/3 oz cashew nuts, toasted

Slice the chicken into finger-length strips.
Heat the oil in a wok or a frying pan and fry the pepper, chicken and garlic over a high heat for about 2 minutes. Add the fish sauce, oyster sauce and sugar and continue to cook, stirring, until the chicken is tender and all the ingredients are evenly glazed.

Stir in the cashew nuts and the spring onions. Serve immediately.

PAT RAFTER

Pat's mother Jocelyn always makes this for him when he comes home from a trip. It is both easy and delicious.

Apricot Chicken

SERVES 4

1.5 kg/3 ¹/₂ lb chicken, cooked
  and cut into eight pieces
425 ml/15 oz can apricot nectar
1 packet French onion soup
1 small packet flaked almonds

Prepare a very hot oven or grill.
Heat nectar and soup together, stirring until thickened. Add chicken pieces.
Roast almonds in oven or under grill for a few minutes.
Serve chicken on a bed of boiled rice or noodles, with almonds sprinkled over the top.

Poultry

Chicken Filo Pie

Allow chicken to cool, then bone and skin and shred into a large pie dish.

Combine the mascarpone, cream, salt and pepper in a large bowl. Blend until thoroughly mixed; add the mushrooms, and pour over the chicken in the pie dish.

Stir all the ingredients together and set aside.

Preheat the oven to 190°C/375°F/gas mark 5.

Melt the butter. When the foam subsides, brush each sheet of filo pastry with butter, using a pastry brush. Lay the sheets across the top of the pie, alternating them in different directions so there are no gaps or filling. As you lay each sheet, brush the top before you lay the next buttered sheet on top. Fold over any edges with the buttering brush.

Bake the pie in the oven for 20 minutes, then remove and brush the top with more melted butter.

Return to the oven and turn the temperature down to 180°C/350°F/gas mark 4 for a further 15–20 minutes or until the pastry is beginning to brown at the edges. (*Watch carefully at this point* because filo pastry looks raw for ages and then goes a burnt brown very quickly.)

When the pie is ready, remove from oven and allow to stand for 10–15 minutes before cutting and serving. (This allows the cream cheese to reset slightly.)

Serve with fresh french beans, cooked *al dente*, and new potatoes garnished with fresh mint and basil.

350 g/12 oz chicken, parboiled for 30 minutes
225 g/8 oz mascarpone cream cheese
150 ml/5 fl oz double cream
salt and freshly ground black pepper
1 teaspoon dried mixed herbs
225 g/8 oz mushrooms, cleaned and roughly sliced
50 g/2 oz butter
8 sheets of filo pastry

I hope this is OK. It's actually a very easy, economical and speedy dish to make that looks really impressive at dinner parties. I think this is a brilliant idea of yours and I wish you, the school and the pupils all the luck you deserve.

lotsa luck
Lucas.

Claridge's Chicken Pie

SERVES 4

1 x 1.35 kg/3 lb chicken
salt and freshly ground black
   pepper
2 tablespoons oil
100 g/4 oz butter
1 onion, chopped
100 g/4 oz plain flour
1.2 litres/2 pints chicken stock
100 g/4 oz button mushrooms
75 g/3 oz streaky bacon, diced
125 ml/4 fl oz double cream
a pinch of chopped parsley
4 hardboiled quail's eggs
300 g/10 oz puff pastry
1 egg, beaten, to glaze

Cut the chicken into even-sized pieces. Season with salt and pepper.

Heat the oil in a sauté pan and add the chicken pieces. Lightly brown them on both sides, then remove from the pan. Add the butter and onion and sweat slowly until the onion has softened.

Add the flour and mix to make a roux. Cook until it becomes a sandy colour. Slowly add the stock, mixing thoroughly, and cook for about 10 minutes to obtain a smooth sauce. Add the chicken pieces.

Sauté the mushrooms and the bacon in a separate pan, then add to the chicken in the sauce. Cook for about 15 minutes, then add the cream and cook for a further 10 minutes. Remove from the heat and allow to cool.

Place the chicken and sauce in a pie dish and add the parsley and hard-boiled eggs.

Roll out the pastry, brush the rim of the pie dish with beaten egg and line with a 1 cm/^{1}/$_2$ in strip of pastry. Press down firmly and brush with more beaten egg.

Cover the pie with a piece of pastry and seal the edges firmly.

Trim off the excess pastry with a knife, knock up the edges and decorate the top with leaves of pastry.

Allow the pie to rest in a cool place for at least 3 hours.

Preheat the oven to 220°C/425°F/gas mark 7.

Place the pie in a bain marie and bake in the oven for about 15–18 minutes or until the pastry is set and lightly coloured and the filling is hot.

Cover the pie with kitchen foil and turn the oven temperature down to 150°C/300°F/gas mark 3. Bake for a further 15–20 minutes.

Serve the hot pie immediately or you may rest it for a while as it will keep hot for quite some time.

The management and staff of Claridge's hotel are very happy, and very flattered, to have been able to contribute a recipe to your special recipe book. This comes to you with our good wishes. The Head Chef, Mr Marjan Lesnik, is very proud to be associated with such a splendid event, and should anyone have any problems with the interpretation of the recipe, he would be happy to give them more detailed advice.

Meat

Stewed Oxtail

SERVES 4

Oxtail takes a long time to cook so it is advisable to cook it partially the day before. It can then be set in a bowl overnight, and the grease will be solidified on top by the next day and can then be easily skimmed off. This makes the stew less rich and much more digestible.

Place the oxtail in a saucepan and cover with cold water. Bring to the boil and simmer, covered, for 15 minutes. Drain to remove scum.

Replace the oxtail in the rinsed-out pan and add the vegetables, salt, pepper and spices and herbs if used. Cover with fresh cold water.

Bring to the boil, then simmer for about $2\frac{1}{2}$ hours until tender.

Add the lemon juice and serve on a hot dish with croûtons or snippets of toast.

I oxtail, jointed into pieces
I large onion, sliced
3 carrots, diced
3–4 young turnips, diced
salt and freshly ground black pepper*
3 cloves*
I blade of mace*
$\frac{1}{4}$ teaspoon ground allspice*
I bouquet garni*
I tablespoon lemon juice

*optional

KERI DAVIES
PRODUCER, THE ARCHERS

Here is a recipe for your book. I hope it helps in a small way the important work that you do:

Nelson's Quick Steak in Mustard Sauce

The Archers

Fry the steak (do not grill it) until done to your liking and place briefly in a warm oven while you chuck the cream into the juices in the pan. Stir in the mustard and heat till bubbling.

Pour the sauce over the steak and serve with bread and green salad. Quick, delicious and lethal!

Meat

Braised Meat Balls with Peppers and Tomatoes

SERVES 4

An economical but really delicious recipe, probably best made in the autumn when there is a glut of tomatoes and green peppers.

450 g/1 lb best quality minced beef

225 g/8 oz good pork sausage meat

$\frac{1}{2}$ green pepper, deseeded and finely chopped

1 egg, beaten

1 medium onion, minced or very finely chopped

1 large garlic clove, crushed

1 teaspoon dried mixed herbs

1 tablespoon chopped parsley

2 teaspoons tomato purée

2 slices of bread

salt and freshly ground black pepper

flour for coating

oil for frying

For the sauce

1 small onion, chopped

$\frac{1}{2}$ green pepper, deseeded and chopped

1 x 400 g/14 oz can of Italian tomatoes or 450 g/1 lb ripe plum tomatoes, skinned and chopped

1 garlic clove, crushed

1 teaspoon dried basil

salt and freshly ground black pepper

Make the meatballs: combine the mince, sausage meat, peppers, egg, onion, garlic, herbs and tomato purée in a large mixing bowl. Cut the crusts off the bread, then mash it to crumbs with a fork and mix very thoroughly with the meatball ingredients, using your hands. Season with salt and pepper.

Now take pieces of the mixture – about a tablespoon at a time – and roll each into a small round. You should get about 16–18 altogether. Coat each one lightly with flour, then brown them in the oil in a large frying pan.

Meanwhile, preheat the oven to 190°C/375°F/gas mark 5. When the meatballs are browned, transfer them to a casserole and prepare the sauce: soften the onion and green pepper in the juices remaining in the frying pan for 5 minutes, then add the tomatoes, garlic and basil. Simmer for a couple of minutes. Taste and season with salt and pepper, then pour the sauce over the meatballs in the casserole and cook, covered, in the oven for 45 minutes. Remove the lid and cook for a further 15–20 minutes.

Delicious served on a bed of noodles with a crisp green salad.

To the pupils of Oak Lodge School

Best Wishes and good luck with the recipe book

Nicholas Parsons

Bitokes à la Russe

(Hamburgers with cream sauce)

Combine the minced beef, onions, 40 g/1½ oz of the butter, 1½ teaspoons salt, ⅛ teaspoon pepper and the egg in a mixing bowl and beat vigorously to blend thoroughly. Taste and adjust the seasoning if necessary. Form into patties 2cm/¾ in thick.

Heat 15g/½ oz of the remaining butter and the oil in a frying pan. Add the hamburgers and fry over a medium heat, turning once, until browned and cooked through. Remove to a hot serving dish.

Pour the fat out of the frying pan. Add the stock and boil it down rapidly, scraping up the cooking juices, until reduced almost to a syrup. Pour in the cream and boil it down rapidly for a minute or two until reduced and thickened slightly. Season to taste with salt, pepper, nutmeg and lemon juice.

Remove the pan from the heat and gradually swirl in the remaining butter until absorbed. Stir in the herbs, spoon the sauce over the hamburgers and serve.

675 g/1½ lb lean minced beef
75 g/3 oz onions, finely chopped
75 g/3 oz softened butter
salt and freshly ground black
  pepper
⅛ teaspoon dried thyme
I egg
2 teaspoons oil
75 ml/3 fl oz beef stock
150 ml/5 fl oz double cream
a pinch of freshly grated nutmeg
a dash of lemon juice
2 tablespoons chopped mixed
  herbs, such as parsley, chives,
  tarragon, chervil, parsley

Hope the publication is a great success and raises lots of pennies.

Ronnie Corbett

Traditional Cornish Pasty

225 g/8 oz chuck steak

1 medium onion

225 g/8 oz potatoes and swede
(called turnip in Cornwall)

salt and freshly ground black
pepper

300 g/10 oz shortcrust pastry

a knob of butter

beaten egg or milk to glaze
(optional)

*P*reheat oven to 200°C/400°F/gas mark 6

Chop the meat, onion, potatoes and swede into very small pieces. Roll out the pastry and cut out 4 equal rounds. Place filling on one half of each circle in this order – mixed potatoes and swede, meat, then onion. Season. Place a small piece of butter on top of each, moisten the edges of the pastry and fold over mixture. Press the edges together firmly and crimp.

Place the pasties on a baking tray. Make a ventilating hole in each. Brush with beaten egg or milk if glaze is required. Bake the pasties in the oven for about 30 minutes or until pale brown. Turn down heat to 180°C/350°F/gas mark 4 and bake for a further 25–30 minutes (Cover with foil if becoming too brown).

P.S. A little moisture (stock) can be added, but very carefully or juices will run out (called 'come abroad' in Cornwall). Vegetables only can be used in vegetarian pasties e.g. onions, leeks, swede, grated carrot, potatoes.

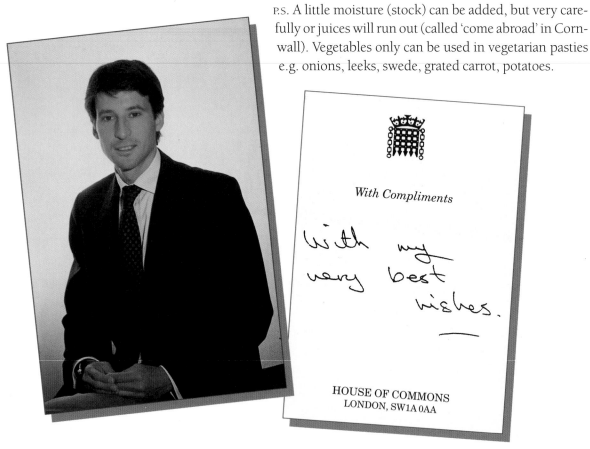

With Compliments

With my very best wishes.

HOUSE OF COMMONS
LONDON, SW1A 0AA

I am delighted to send you one of my wife's recipes for the book you are compiling. This comes with my warmest wishes for the future well-being of the school and its pupils and staff.

Myra's Stuffed Aubergines

SERVES 8

Put the minced beef into a heavy saucepan, cover with water, bring to the boil and then simmer for 5 minutes. Pour off the liquid, then add the onions, garlic, herbs and tomato juice. Mix the Bovril and Worcestershire sauce with a little hot water and add to the mince. Simmer for 45 minutes or until tender.

Preheat the oven to 180°C/350°F/gas mark 4.

Place the aubergines in water and simmer until the skins start to wrinkle (do not overcook). Cut in half lengthwise, scoop out the flesh and mix with the minced beef. Fill the aubergine shells with the mixture and bake in the oven for 30 minutes, or until tender. Sprinkle with the breadcrumbs and place under a hot grill to brown. Serve at once.

900 g/2 lb lean minced beef
225 g/8 oz onions, chopped
1 garlic clove, crushed
1 tablespoon dried mixed herbs
300 ml/10 fl oz tomato juice
a dash of Worcestershire sauce
3 teaspoons Bovril
freshly ground black pepper
8 aubergines
100 g/4 oz fresh white
   breadcrumbs

Spare Ribs

900 g/2 lb pork spare ribs
salt and freshly ground black
    pepper
1 onion, chopped
1 mugful of tomato ketchup
³/₄ mug of red wine vinegar
3 tablespoons Worcestershire
    sauce
3 tablespoons soft dark brown
    sugar
1 teaspoon made English
    mustard

Preheat the oven to 180°C/350°F/gas mark 4.
    Place the ribs in a roasting tin, sprinkle with salt and pepper and roast for 30 minutes. Drain and transfer to an ovenproof dish.

Fry the onion lightly in a little of the fat in a saucepan until soft, then drain off any excess fat and add all the remaining ingredients. Bring to the boil, stirring constantly.

Pour the mixture over the ribs and leave to marinate for several hours, ideally overnight. Turn the ribs occasionally.

Preheat the oven to 150°C/300°F/gas mark 2. Cook the ribs for 1½–2 hours or until tender. If you like them crispy, turn up the oven temperature to 200°C/400°F/gas mark 6 for the last 30 minutes.

Chilli con Carne

450 g/1 lb onions, chopped
olive oil for frying
4 garlic cloves, crushed
1.35 kg/3 lb lean minced beef
4 teaspoons Schwartz chilli
    essence
1 tablespoon ground cumin
1 tablespoon ground coriander
1 tablespoon dried oregano
3 x 400 g/14 oz cans of red
    kidney beans
3 x 400 g/14 oz cans of
    tomatoes
450 g/1 lb mushrooms, chopped
1 small can of red sweet
    pimentos
about 575 ml/1 pint chicken
    stock
150 ml/5 fl oz tarragon vinegar
3 tablespoons soft light brown
    sugar
100 g/4 oz cooking chocolate
tomato paste

Fry the onions in a little olive oil in a large saucepan until translucent. Add the garlic and fry for 1 further minute. Add the mince together with all the seasonings. Add the kidney beans, tomatoes, mushrooms, and pimentos. Pour the chicken stock over the ingredients; there should be enough to cover. Add the vinegar, sugar, chocolate and tomato paste.

Simmer gently for about 3 hours, stirring occasionally.

Serve the chilli with plain boiled rice or pasta. Grated cheese sprinkled over the top of each serving is a good addition.

This dish freezes very well, and gains strength of flavour.

Meat

The Lenny Henry Killer Chilli

SERVES 4

*P*lace the rabbit's foot round your neck (you're going to need all the luck you can get because I certainly don't know what I'm doing).

Fry the onions and green peppers in the butter until they are fairly translucent (that means see-through, thicky). Add the minced beef and fry until brown.

Add the tomatoes and stir for a couple of minutes until the mixture is bubbling noisily. Add the tomato purée and stir until the sauce thickens. Add all the spices and herbs with the mushrooms and stir for 2 minutes.

Add the kidney beans and give a good stir. Add a dash of Tabasco, crumble in the stock cubes, add the wine and stir again. Simmer over a low heat for about 1 hour, stirring occasionally, until a lovely dark brown colour and quite thick. Skim off any fat with a spoon.

Yum Yum in my tum!

Serve with plain boiled rice or pitta bread.

1 lucky rabbit's foot!
2 large onions, chopped
2 green peppers, deseeded and
    chopped
100 g/4 oz butter
450 g/1 lb minced beef
1 x 400 g/14 oz can of Italian
    tomatoes
1 tablespoon tomato purée
chilli powder (mild or not
    depending on whether your
    tongue is made of
    leather!)
a pinch of ground mixed spice
a pinch of ground cloves
a pinch of dried oregano
100 g/4 oz mushrooms,
    chopped
1 x 400 g/14 oz can of kidney
    beans
2 beef stock cubes

Green Beef Curry

SERVES 4

*T*his curry is fairly hot. If you feel you can cope with a little more heat, stir in some extra green curry paste to taste.

675 g/1 1/2 lb rump steak
1 tablespoon oil
1 tablespoon green curry paste
1/2 teaspoon ground cinnamon
1 tablespoon fish sauce
150 ml/5 fl oz coconut milk
grated zest of 1/2 lime
1 teaspoon soft light brown
   sugar
steamed fragrant rice, to serve
shredded Kaffir lime leaves or
   coriander leaves, to garnish

Trim the steak of any fat and cut into finger-length strips. Heat the oil in a wok or frying pan and fry the meat in batches over a high heat to give it a good brown colour. Add more oil if necessary.

Return the meat to the pan, add all the remaining ingredients and cook, stirring, for 3 minutes or until the sauce has reduced slightly and the meat is tender. Garnish with Kaffir lime or coriander leaves and serve with fragrant rice.

ED MIRVISH

Annie's Cabbage Rolls 'Sweet & Sour'

*T*his is my favourite recipe – one of my wife Anne's.

1 medium cabbage (12 leaves)
1 large egg, beaten
1 grated onion
1 grated carrot
5 tbsp water
pinch of salt and peper
450 g/1 lb medium ground beef
1/2 cup uncooked rice
small quantity of oil for frying

For the sauce
2 cans (750 g/28 oz) tomatoes
50 g/2 oz lemon juice
5 tbsp brown sugar
1 celery stalk, finely chopped
1 bay leaf
1 cup beef stock

Preheat the oven to 180°C/350°F/gas mark 4.

Blanch the cabbage leaves in boiling water for one minute, drain and leave to one side.

Mix egg, onion, carrot, water, salt, pepper and beef together, and fry quickly in the oil to seal. Boil the rice in water until tender and add to the beef mixture.

Make the sauce by putting all the ingredients in a large saucepan and bringing them gently to boiling point.

Spread each of the cabbage leaves flat, vein side up, and place a dessertspoonful of beef and rice mixture on each leaf. Wrap tightly to form a neat parcel. Pack the twelve parcels tightly in a casserole and pour the sauce over the top.

Cover and bake in the oven for 1 hour.

Steak and Kidney Pie

SERVES 4

Preheat the oven to 200°C/400°F/gas mark 6.

Cut the steak into cubes and cut up the kidney, removing the core. Heat the oil in a flameproof casserole and fry the steak and kidney to seal, then add the onion and fry until translucent. Sprinkle over the flour then place the casserole, uncovered, in the oven for 5 minutes to allow the flour to soak up the fat.

Then mix in the tomato purée. Add the stock, wine, mushrooms and herbs. Bring to the boil, then simmer for 1 hour.

Season with salt and pepper and put into a pie dish.

Roll out the pastry to form a lid. Cut a strip of pastry and place round the edge of the dish, brush with water and put the pastry lid on top, pressing the edges to seal Knock up the sides with a knife and decorate the top with leaves made from the pastry trimmings. Brush the pastry with egg and bake in the oven for 30–35 minutes or until the pastry is golden-brown.

675 g/1 1/2 lb stewing steak
175 g/6 oz ox kidney
2 tablespoons oil
1 onion, sliced
3 tablespoons plain flour
2 tablespoons tomato purée
850 ml/1 1/2 pints beef stock
150 ml/5 fl oz red wine
225 g/8 oz mushrooms, sliced
2 tablespoons chopped parsley and basil
salt and freshly ground black pepper
375 g/12 oz puff pastry
beaten egg, to glaze

Steak and Kidney Pie is also a favourite of Edward Fox, who serves it with mashed potatoes and Brussels sprouts.

With warmest Good wishes.
Yours Sincerely
Edward Fox.

Fillet of Beef with Mango Glaze

SERVES 4

4 x 110 g/4 oz beef fillet steaks,
   trimmed
1 large, ripe mango
1 teaspoon fruit chutney
575 ml/1 pint veal stock
2 shallots, finely chopped
50 ml/2 fl oz Madeira
2 small carrots, roughly chopped
1 large onion, roughly chopped
1 garlic clove, finely diced
1 teaspoon mild curry powder
1 teaspoon sultanas
a pinch of ground ginger
1 egg yolk
75 ml/3 fl oz extra virgin olive
   oil
2 large leeks
3 tablespoons chopped
   deseeded tomato

*P*reheat the oven to 200°C/400°F/gas mark 6.
Tie the beef fillets with string around the centre to ensure they keep their shape while cooking.

Peel the mango, then cut in half. Cut half into strips 5cm × 2mm/2 × $\frac{1}{8}$ in; reserve for the garnish. Purée the other half of the mango in a food processor or blender. Stir in the chutney.

Bring the stock to the boil and boil until reduced by three-quarters.

Sweat the shallots in a covered non-stick pan over a low heat until translucent. Deglaze with the Madeira, boil to reduce by half, then pour in the stock. In a separate pan sweat the carrots, onions, garlic, curry powder, sultanas and ginger for 5 minutes over a low heat. Cover with water and cook for 30 minutes. Add to the chutney and mango mixture.

Heat a roasting tin on the top of the stove, season the beef fillets and seal on both sides in the hot tin. Roast in the oven for 12 minutes.

Meanwhile, in a large bowl whisk the egg yolk with 1 tablespoon warm water until light and frothy. Add to the chutney mixture and mix well. Remove the beef from the oven and spoon a little of the mango glaze over each fillet. Place under a hot grill for approximately 45 seconds.

Heat the oil in a large pan until smoking. Discard the green parts of the leeks and cut the white parts into thin strips. Fry until golden brown. Drain on absorbent paper.

Add the reserved mango strips and the chopped tomato to the sauce and warm slightly. Spoon a pool of sauce on to each plate and place a glazed fillet steak on top. Garnish with the strips of leek.

Meat

I find this is very easy to make for a dinner party because it takes hardly any time to prepare and doesn't need to be cooked until everyone has arrived – a bonus for anyone who has burnt the food while waiting for an unfortunately delayed guest.

I would usually serve this on a large serving plate with mashed potatoes, green beans and baked tomatoes.

Rack of Lamb with Garlic and Rosemary

SERVES 6

Carefully remove the 'eye' of the lamb meat from the bone. Finely chop the rosemary leaves and slice the cloves of garlic and rub these into the meat. Season the meat with salt and pepper, place it in a flat dish and pour over enough oil to cover it completely. Tightly cover the bowl and leave it overnight in a cool place.

Preheat the oven to 230°C/450°F/gas mark 8.

Bring the meat to room temperature. Pour a little of the oil from the bowl into a roasting tin and heat. Add the meat, and roast in the oven for 10 minutes.

Meanwhile, heat the remaining garlic and rosemary oil, drain the beans and add to the warm oil.

Remove the meat from the oven and allow to stand in a warm, but not hot, place. Scrape off any crispy bits from the roasting tin and add to the beans. Pour the beans on to a warmed serving plate, carve the meat and place the slices either on top or to the side of the beans. Serve with tomatoes, green beans and mashed potatoes.

4 racks of lamb
1 large bunch of rosemary
4 garlic cloves
olive oil
2 x 400 g/14 oz cans of flageolet beans
salt and freshly ground black pepper

Meat

BETTY DRIVER

Hotpot

25 g/1 oz dripping
675 g/1¹/₂ lb neck of lamb, cubed
1 large or 2 medium onions,
    roughly chopped
1 tablespoon plain flour
425 ml/³/₄ pint light stock or hot
    water
1 tablespoon Worcestershire
    sauce
1 bayleaf
25 g/1 oz butter
675 g/1¹/₂ lb potatoes, peeled
    and thinly sliced
salt and freshly ground black
    pepper

Preheat the oven to 170°C/325°F/gas mark 3.

Melt the dripping in a heavy-bottomed frying pan over a high heat until the fat smokes. Seal the lamb and continue frying until nicely browned. Remove the pieces from the pan to a deep casserole or divide among 4 individual high-sided, ovenproof dishes.

Turn down the heat to medium. Fry the onions in the pan juices, adding a little more dripping if necessary. When the onions are soft and starting to brown, sprinkle on the flour and stir in to soak up the fat and the juices. As the flour paste starts to colour, start adding stock or water a few tablespoons at a time, stirring vigorously to avoid lumps. Gradually add the remaining liquid. Bring to a simmer, stirring constantly, add the Worcestershire sauce and season to taste with salt and pepper.

Pour the onions and liquid over the meat and mix well. Tuck in the bayleaf (tear into 4 pieces if making individual hotpots).

Arrange the potatoes over the meat in overlapping layers, seasoning each layer. Dot the top layer of potato with the butter.

Cover the dish and cook on the top shelf of the oven for 2 hours. Uncover and cook for a further 30 minutes. If the potatoes are not brown by this point, turn up the oven and cook for a further 15 minutes, on finish off under the grill, brushing the potato slices with more butter if they look too dry.

Meat

Tian d'Agneau Rôti, Sauce Céléri à la Menthe Fraîche

(Pot-roasted loin of lamb with minted celery sauce)

SERVES 6

*P*reheat the oven to 190°C/375°F/gas mark 5.

Season the lamb, which must be at room temperature, with salt and pepper and rub with chopped rosemary and thyme. Sauté briefly in a roasting tin in the oil and butter to seal in the juices. Add the celeriac and celery with the garlic. Add the wine with a spoonful of water.

Roast in the oven, covered, for 10 minutes, then baste and continue to roast, uncovered, for 8–10 minutes for medium cooked meat.

Remove from the oven and allow to cool for 4–5 minutes, then wrap in kitchen foil to keep warm. Add the stock to the tin and cook gently, uncovered, for 35 minutes on top of the stove while continually skimming off the impurities. Then press through a fine strainer, to extract the maximum of juice and some of the vegetable flesh to thicken the sauce. Add the mint, infuse for 10–12 minutes, then strain the sauce again before serving.

Preheat the oven to 220°C/425°F/gas mark 7.

Make the potato base, fry the onions in the oil until golden brown and add the warm shredded potatoes, salt and pepper. Stir constantly over a low heat until hot and thoroughly mixed, then cool and shape into a round on a greased baking sheet. Bake in the oven for 5–6 minutes, then transfer to a serving dish.

Slice the lamb thinly, arrange on the potato base in a circular fashion, and coat with the sauce. Garnish with hot minted vegetables and mint leaves.

For the pot-roast

1.5 kg/3$\frac{1}{2}$ lb fillets of loin of lamb
salt and freshly ground black pepper
chopped rosemary and thyme
50 ml/2 fl oz oil
100 g/4 oz butter
300 g/10 oz celeriac, peeled and cut into 1 cm/$\frac{1}{2}$ in cubes
200 g/7 oz celery, chopped
1–2 garlic cloves
1 tablespoon dry white wine
1.2 litres/2 pints lamb or chicken stock
50 g/2 oz bunch of fresh mint, roughly chopped

For the potato base

150 g/5 oz onions, finely chopped
100 ml/3$\frac{1}{2}$ fl oz ground nut or vegetable (not olive) oil
1.2 kg/2$\frac{1}{2}$ lb cooked jacket potatoes, peeled and shredded
salt and freshly ground black pepper

vegetables steamed with mint, to garnish

GREG NORMAN

Australian Meat Pie

SERVES 4–5

25 g/1 oz butter or margarine
2 small onions, finely chopped
450 g/2 lb chopped sirloin
2 tablespoon plain flour
2¹/₂ cups beef bouillon or stock
salt and pepper to taste
1 teaspoon dried thyme
2 tablespoons Worcestershire sauce
¹/₄ cup chopped parsley
pinch nutmeg
pastry (store bought pastry works very well)
1 egg, slightly beaten

*M*elt butter in a saucepan. Add onions and fry over moderate heat until onions soften. Add beef and fry, pressing down with fork until beef is browned, drain. Sprinkle flour over beef, stir and continue cooking for a further 2 minutes. Remove pan from heat. Gradually add stock. Return pan to the heat and stir constantly until mixture boils and thickens. Add all remaining ingredients. Cover pan and simmer over a low heat for 30 minutes. Line pie tin with pastry. Prick the base several times with a fork. Using a sharp knife, trim off excess pastry. Spoon filling in. Brush around edge with beaten egg. Top with pastry pressing edges together. Cut a hole in centre of pie. Brush with remaining egg. Cook at 200°C/400°F/gas mark 6 degrees for 25 minutes or until crust is golden brown

MOHAMED AL FAYED

Ritzy Beef

SERVES 4

4 filet mignons, cut 2.5 cm/1 in thick
salt and freshly ground black pepper
4 tablespoons butter (divided as below)
1 shallot, minced
100 g/4 oz fresh mushrooms, quartered
125 ml/4 fl oz beef stock
125 ml/4 fl oz Madeira, or additional beef stock
chopped parsley, to garnish (optional)

*S*eason the beef with salt and pepper to taste. Then, in a medium sauté pan, melt 2 tablespoons of the butter. When the butter stops foaming, sauté the filets for 6–7 minutes on each side, for a medium-rare steak. Remove the meat from the pan and pour off any grease.

In a small sauté pan, melt the remaining butter. Sauté the shallot for 2 minutes. Add the mushrooms and cook for 3 minutes until lightly browned. Set aside.

Add the stock to the meat pan and boil rapidly, scraping up the browned bits, until 2 tablespoons remain. Add the Madeira and boil rapidly until the sauce thickens, approximately 2–3 minutes. Put the mushrooms back in and simmer for 1 minute more. Serve the steaks with the sauce over the top and garnish with parsley, if liked.

Vegetables

Vegetable Dolmas

SERVES 6

*D*olmas are stuffed vegetables. They are prepared differently according to regions within the Middle East. When stuffed with rice, dolmas can be enjoyed either hot or cold. If chopped meat is included, they are preferably served warm.

A variety of vegetables grown in the Jordan Valley are suitable for dolmas: aubergines, tomatoes, courgettes, peppers, carrots, cabbage and vine leaves.

Make the sauce: combine all the ingredients and mix with 570ml/1 pint water. Heat gently to reduce slightly. Set aside.

Cut the ends off the courgettes and reserve. Scoop out the courgette flesh. Wash the shells well.

Soak the rice in warm water for 30 minutes, then wash and drain.

Sauté the onion in the butter in a frying pan over a medium heat, add the mince and sauté for 7 minutes, then add the rice. Continue cooking for 5 minutes.

Add the herbs and tomato and cook for 2 minutes. Season with salt and pepper and add 75ml/3fl oz water. Simmer for 5 minutes, then remove from heat and allow to cool.

Stuff the courgettes with this mixture and replace the ends, securing with cocktail sticks.

Place the stuffed courgettes in a casserole. Pour over the sauce and cook for about 40 minutes or until tender. (Check after 30 minutes to see if more water is needed.) Serve hot, garnished with parsley or dill.

12 medium courgettes
300 g/10 oz risotto rice
1 medium onion, finely grated
50 g/2 oz butter
225 g/8 oz minced beef or
    lamb
1 tablespoon chopped parsley
1 tablespoon chopped mint
1 tablespoon chopped dill
1 medium tomato, skinned and
    deseeded
salt and freshly ground black
    pepper

For the sauce
1 tablespoon melted butter
1 tablespoon tomato paste
1 large tomato, skinned and
    finely chopped
salt and freshly ground black
    pepper

Vegetables

Sun-Dried Tomato Risotto

SERVES 4

4 tbsp olive oil, from the jar of tomatoes

2 garlic cloves, peeled and chopped

1 small onion, peeled and chopped

250 g/8 oz arborio rice

4 tbsp sun-dried tomatoes, cut into small pieces

125 g/4 oz small button mushrooms

750 ml/1 1/4 pints hot chicken stock

4 heaped tbsp parsley, freshly chopped

50 g/2 oz freshly grated Parmesan

salt and pepper

parmesan shavings, to serve

Heat the oil in a saucepan and gently fry the garlic and onion for a couple of minutes.

Add the rice, stir well to coat with the oil, then add the tomatoes and mushrooms. Cook for a minute or two, until everything is well coated.

One ladle at a time, gradually add the hot stock, stirring well with each addition. After about 15 minutes, add the parsley and continue to simmer until the grains are just cooked. (You may not need all the stock.)

Add the Parmesan, season to taste with salt and pepper, then cover and allow to stand, off the heat, for about 10 minutes. Sprinkle the Parmesan shaving over the top and serve.

recipe reproduced from Feasting on Herbs, *published by Kyle Cathie Ltd*

Very best wishes to Oak Lodge School from Sue Lawrence (BBC Masterchef 1991)

ANITA RODDICK

I am delighted to learn of your work and would like to share with you and the school one of my favourite sayings:

'You don't have to be big, you just have to be brave!'

Dutch Potato Broccoli

SERVES 4–6

Preheat the oven to 180°C/350°F/gas mark 4.

Cook the potatoes in the cream and water until tender. Do not drain. Thicken the liquid with the cornflour mixed with a small amount of water.

Meanwhile, chop the broccoli into 2.5–5 cm/1–2 in chunks and cook until fork tender. Add the potato mixture, along with the peanut butter and onion. Stir well to mix.

Put into a buttered 3 litre/5 pint casserole and sprinkle generously with Parmesan cheese.

Bake in the oven for 30 minutes.

Anita Roddick

3 large boiling potatoes, peeled and diced
350 ml/12 fl oz double cream
1 tablespoon cornflour
450 g/1 lb fresh broccoli
100 g/4 oz smooth peanut butter
1 onion, finely chopped
freshly grated Parmesan cheese

DAME JUDI DENCH

Potato Cakes

*T*ake any left-over mashed potatoes and put into a good-sized bowl. Sieve plain flour into the potatoes, mixing as you go, until you have a stiff dough. Add salt and pepper to taste.

Roll out on a well-floured board to 1 cm/¹/₂ in thickness. Cut into squares or other shapes, such as diamonds, triangles or circles, and place on a dry hot griddle or in a heavy frying pan. Cook until brown on both sides, then split and butter.

These are also delicious with bacon.

Oak Lodge does a marvellous job, and I wish you every success with the book.

Judi Dench

Vegetables

I enclose a recipe that is simplicity itself, but above all, I send you my best wishes for your efforts to find the bright places in your child. They are always there somewhere as you know, even if the traditional educational system has difficulty finding them.

I share with you the knowledge that Jonathan carries many jewels, and I know that with your help he will learn to express them.

I send my best wishes to you and to all those working in the Autistic Department of Oak Lodge School.

Champ
SERVES 4

10 spring onions, or 2 leeks
1/2 cup of milk
675g/1 1/2 lb freshly cooked
    potatoes
salt and freshly ground black
    pepper

Cook the spring onions or leeks, green part as well as white, in the milk until tender. Drain and reserve the milk. Mash the potatoes, season to taste with salt and pepper and add the spring onions or leeks. Beat well together and add enough of the hot milk to make the mixture creamy and smooth.

Place the mixture in a deep, warmed dish. Make a well in the centre and pour in the butter. The mashed potato should be dipped in the pool of butter when serving.

Champ can also be made with chopped parsley, chives, young nettle tops or young green peas. If the peas are used, they are kept whole and added last. For a supper dish, scrambled eggs are often served in the centre and sprinkled with chopped parsley. This dish will kindle the coldest heart.

Carrott Curry

SERVES 4–6

Place the carrots in a saucepan with the orange juice, salt, and enough water just to cover. Simmer for about 5 minutes.

In a large deep frying pan, heat the butter or ghee and add all the spices. Heat for a few minutes, then add the carrots in their liquid, the raisins and the banana, very thinly sliced. Simmer the curry over a slow heat for about 30 minutes.

If the liquid seems too thin, ladle some of it into a cup and mix well with a little cornflour to make a smooth, thin paste. Return to the curry and stir in. Heat for a few minutes more and the curry is ready to serve.

675–900 g/1 1/2–2 lb carrots, sliced diagonally
225 ml/8 fl oz fresh orange juice
1 teaspoon salt
water
4 tablespoons butter or ghee
4–5 cardamon pods (seeds only)
1 1/2 teaspoons ground turmeric
1 1/2 teaspoons mustard seeds
4 whole cloves
1 tablespoon cumin seeds
1/2 teaspoon curry powder (optional)
2–3 tablespoons raisins
1 ripe banana
1 1/2 tablespoons cornflour

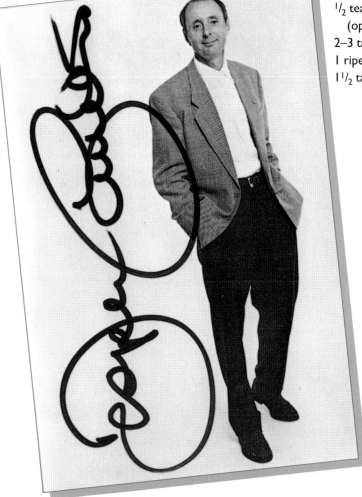

Vegetables

Onion and Thyme Tart

SERVES 6

This tart was part of a *Vogue* feature on picnics, but it is wonderful for any occasion.

The consistency of the onion and thyme custard is truly exquisite, very lightly set, and nice and deep. At a smart picnic you can serve this with a leafy salad accompaniment, as a first or as a main course.

250 g/9 oz puff pastry
20 g/³/₄ oz unsalted butter
1.3 kg/1 lb 10 oz white onions, sliced
1 teaspoon salt
200 ml/7 fl oz milk
2 large egg yolks
1 large egg
1 heaped tablespoon freshly grated Parmesan
1 teaspoon coarsely chopped thyme
freshly ground black pepper

Preheat the oven to 180°C/350°F/gas mark 4.

Roll out the pastry 12 mm/¹/₈ in thick and use to line a loose-bottomed 20 cm/8 in cake tin, 6 cm/2¹/₂in deep. Run the rolling pin over the rim to remove the excess pastry. Prick the base all over with a fork and line with foil and baking beans. Bake blind for about 25 minutes or until lightly golden. Remove the foil and beans.

Meanwhile, heat the butter in a medium saucepan, add the onions and salt and cook, covered, over a low heat for 40 minutes, until very soft. Stir them occasionally to make sure they are not sticking.

In a bowl, whisk together all the remaining ingredients and season with pepper, then stir in the onions. Pour this filling into the baked case.

Bake in the oven for 30–35 minutes or until the filling is set and lightly golden on the surface. Allow to cool, then trim the pastry in line with the filling. Serve at room temperature.

Best wishes
Annie Bell

Pommes Anna with Leeks and Provolone

SERVES 4

Finely sliced potatoes are layered with leeks and cheese, which adhere together into a cake. Traditionally butter is added between each layer, which is unnecessary here due to the fat in the cheese. An omelette pan or small frying pan works perfectly, and the whole thing is inverted once cooked. Usually Pommes Anna will have a crisp exterior; accidentally, when I was trying to achieve this, I turned out a dish as soft on the outside as it was in the centre. As the dish, intended for four, bit by bit disappeared into the mouths of two, I decided it should stay this way.

Wash the leeks, halve them lengthwise and chop them, and mince the garlic. Melt 35g/1¹⁄₄oz of the butter in a frying pan and cook the leeks, garlic, thyme and seasoning and 5 minutes until soft, though not coloured.

Preheat the oven to 190°C/375°F/gas mark 5. Peel the potatoes and slice transparently thin, using a mandolin if you have one, discarding the end slices. Choose a frying pan with a heat-resistant handle and place a square of foil on the base so that when the dish is turned out it does not stick. Butter the pan and foil very well, using about 20g/³⁄₄oz butter.

Lay a layer of potato slices in concentric circles on the base, starting with a circle in the centre and then working towards the outside. This layer should be quite thick. Sprinkle over a little salt, scatter over half of the leeks and half of the cheese. Repeat the layers until all the ingredients are used up: there should be three layers of potato, two of filling. Dot the surface with the remaining butter and cover with foil. Bake this for 1 hour. Loosen the base using a flexible palette knife and invert it on to a plate.

450 g/1 lb leeks, trimmed weight
1 garlic clove
45 g/1³⁄₄ oz unsalted butter and
    20 g/³⁄₄ oz to butter the pan
1 teaspoon of thyme
salt, pepper
780 g/1³⁄₄ lb potatoes
50 g/2 oz Provolone, grated
50 g/2 oz Gruyere, grated

Recipe reprinted from Evergreen:
Classic Vegetarian Cookery *(Bantam Press)*

Asparagus and Broccoli Charlotte

SERVES 4

30 thin green asparagus spears
30 thin white asparagus spears
250 g/8¹/₂ oz broccoli heads
4 eggs
300ml/10 fl oz natural, low-fat
  fromage frais
sea salt and freshly milled white
  pepper

for the sauce
1 potato, peeled and roughly
  chopped
575 ml/1 pint fresh orange juice
1 cardamon pod (bean), crushed
¹/₂ clove garlic, finely diced
  (minced)
¹/₂ bay leaf
1 teaspoon fresh tarragon,
  chopped
2 teaspoons natural, low-fat
  fromage frais

to garnish
1 tomato, sliced

To make the sauce, place all the ingredients except the tarragon and the fromage frais in a pan and reduce over a high heat by two-thirds, about 20 minutes. Stir in the fromage frais and pass through a fine sieve. Season to taste.

To make the charlottes, lightly grease 4 ramekins and line with grease-proof (wax) paper. Cut away the woody ends from the asparagus, then trim the tips into 4 cm/1¹/₂ in lengths; reserve the stalks for the mousse. Using string, tie the tips into bundles and blanch in plenty of salted water for 1 minute, then refresh under cold running water and drain. Discard the strings. Cut half the broccoli heads into florets and blanch as before.

To make the mousse, cook the other half of the broccoli heads with the asparagus stalks until tender. Refresh under cold running water, drain, then combine with the eggs and fromage frais in a liquidizer or food processor and blend until smooth. Season to taste.

Preheat the oven to 180°C/350°F/gas mark 4. Line the ramekins with asparagus tips, alternating green and white spears. Spoon the mousse mixture into the ramekins and smooth level. Place the broccoli florets around the top. Cook in a *bain marie* in the oven for 25 minutes until slightly risen. Leave to rest for 5 minutes. Meanwhile, reheat the sauce and stir in the chopped tarragon. Plunge each ramekin into hot water for 30 seconds up to the rim and turn out the charlottes on to a plate. Surround with a little of the sauce and slices of tomato. Serve immediately.

Vegetables

Grilled Mediterranean Vegetables

SERVES 6

This dish is the only way to make something as boring as a courgette taste wonderful and it has the advantage of being good hot, great lukewarm, delicious cold and irresistible the next day.

Preheat the grill, grill pan, barbecue or oven broiler to maximum.

Cut the fennel into thick slices, leaving some stalk end on each slice to hold the leaves together.

Use a swivel peeler to remove the thin outer membrane of the peppers. Then cut them into sections down the creases, remove the pith and seeds and peel any edges previously missed. Cut each section in half.

In a large bowl, turn all the vegetables in oil to coat.

Arrange the vegetables on the grill pan or a foil-lined grill tray.

Grill to char both sides. Remove the vegetables as they are done.

Serve warm or cold, drizzled with additional olive oil, seasoned generously with sea salt and freshly ground black pepper and garnished with fresh basil and a few black olives.

2 heads of fennel

1 large red pepper

1 large yellow pepper

2 small aubergines, sliced lengthwise into 5mm/^{1}/$_4$ in thick strips

2 courgettes, sliced lengthwise into 5 mm/^{1}/$_4$ in thick strips

6 spring onions, trimmed and sliced in half lengthwise if thick

6 medium field mushrooms, tough stems removed

to garnish
fresh basil
squashy black olives

Chilli Non Carne

SERVES 4

The classic chilli con carne – made with vegetable steak chunks instead of meat! It can be served either with rice or with baked potatoes and a tossed salad of your choice. Mexican corn bread is another delicious accompaniment.

1 large onion, sliced finely
2 tbsp olive oil
2 cloves garlic, crushed
1½ tsp chilli powder, or to taste
250 g/8 oz vegetarian steak chunks
450 ml/¾ pint vegetable stock
1 x 400 g/14 oz can chopped tomatoes
1 x 400 g/14 oz can red kidney beans, drained
1–2 canned mild green chillies, drained and chopped (optional)
sea salt

Sauté the onion in the hot oil for 3–4 minutes, then add the garlic, chilli powder and steak chunks and stir until well mixed. Brown for 5 minutes, stirring. Add the stock and the tomatoes with their juice, then leave to simmer gently, covered, for 20 minutes.

Add the kidney beans and the chilli if desired, and simmer for a further 15 minutes.

Season to taste with a little salt if necessary, and leave to stand for 10 minutes before serving to allow the flavours to develop.

Nutty Sprouts

SERVES 4

*T*his is a French recipe, which may sound a bit odd, but adds some 'oomph' to the sprouts!

Preheat the oven to 180°C/350°F/gas mark 4.

Peel and skin the chestnuts (removing the skin is easier if the chestnut is plunged into boiling water first for a few minutes).

Cook the chestnuts in boiling water until tender. When they are cool enough to handle, chop them into small pieces.

Remove the outer leaves from the sprouts, make a cross cut in the stem and wash them. Place in a saucepan with sufficient boiling water to cover the bottom (steam them if possible) and cook until almost tender. Drain.

Mix all the ingredients together in a casserole and season with pepper. Cover and cook in the centre of the oven for 10 minutes.

10 sweet chestnuts
450 g/1 lb Brussels sprouts
100 g/4 oz cooked ham, cut into
 1 cm/½ in squares
4 tablespoons plain yoghurt
freshly ground black pepper

Did you know?

The Brussels sprout really is named after the capital city of Belgium where it is said to originate.

Richard Briers

Daily Mail and General Trust plc

Northcliffe House, 2 Derry Street, Kensington, W8 5TT
Telephone: 071-938 6610   Telex: 884243
Fax: 071-937 0043

17th June 1994

Mrs. Caroline Esdaile,
35 Lyndhurst Road,
London NW3 5PE

Dear Mrs. Esdaile,

Thank you for your letter. The only recipe I can offer you is one which I heard on the BBC many years ago - very simple and one of the oldest recipes in existence, it being a favourite of the mediaeval kings.

The recipe has a Welsh name which I cannot remember but which sounds like sleazy socks. The ingredients are olive oil, leeks and white wine. The leeks, having been cleaned, are cut into one inch lengths and sauteed in the olive oil in a large skillet until brown. White wine is then added and the leeks are left to simmer gently until completely soft. They should be eaten with large slices of dark brown bread.

I wish every good will to your children and the success of your school and its very important mission of promoting self-esteem and self confidence without which life cannot be properly lived.

Yours sincerely,

Lord Rothermere

Puddings

*T*hank you for your letter and please find enclosed two of my favourite recipes for the cookery book you are compiling.

I do hope these will help you with the fund raising and may I wish you all the best of luck.

Summer Teaser

SERVES 4

Mix together the lime juice, white wine and crème de cassis in a bowl. Sift in the icing sugar and whisk well to mix. Stir in the chopped mint. Cover and chill in the refrigerator for at least 1 hour.

Rinse the berries and dry them carefully. Divide them among 4 small soup plates or shallow dessert bowls.

Strain the lime mixture and spoon it over the berries.

Dip a dessertspoon in hot water, then scrape it across the surface of the sorbet, rolling the sorbet into the spoon to make a neat shape.

Put the sorbet on top of the berries, add a sprig of mint and serve immediately.

juice of 3 limes
150 ml/15 fl oz Chablis or other
    dry white wine
4 tablespoons crème de cassis
60 g/2 oz icing sugar
2 teaspoons chopped fresh mint
350 g/12 oz mixed summer
    berries, such as raspberries,
    strawberries, blackberries,
    wild strawberries,
    blueberries, loganberries
225 g/8 oz strawberry sorbet
fresh mint sprigs, to decorate

Poached Peaches Served in a Honey Basket with Rosehip Tea and Fig Sorbet

SERVES 4

2.25 litres/4 pints fresh orange juice

2 star anise

4 ripe peaches

50 ml/2 fl oz clear honey

50 g/2 oz raw cane sugar

25 g/1 oz polyunsaturated spread

1 egg white

75 g/3 oz wholemeal flour

8 dried figs

1.1 litres/2 pints rosehip tea

1/2 lemon

To decorate

100 g/4 oz redcurrants, removed from stems, or raspberries

icing sugar, for dusting (optional)

4 mint sprigs

Put the orange juice and star anise into a non-stick pan and bring to the boil. Add the peaches and poach in the liquid until tender. Remove from the pan and leave to cool.

Preheat the oven to 220°C/425°F/gas mark 7.

Using a wooden spoon, mix the honey, sugar and polyunsaturated spread to a smooth paste in a large bowl. Slowly add the egg white and flour, stirring continuously. Spread on a baking sheet in 4 circles, each 10 cm/4 in in diameter and 2 mm/^{1}/$_8$ in thick. Place in the freezer for 5 minutes. Bake in the oven for $4^1/_2$ minutes, then immediately remove from the tray, using a spatula or flat knife, and place in a deep, curved mould or rounded tea cup to form a basket shape. Leave to cool.

Boil the figs in the rosehip tea for about 10 minutes or until soft. Strain off a quarter of the rosehip tea and reserve. Liquidize the figs with the lemon and a little tea until it is the texture of olive oil. Pass through a sieve into a large bowl. Place in the freezer and whisk vigorously every 20 minutes; it will take about 3 hours for the ice crystals to form. Alternatively place in an ice cream maker or *sorbetière* until stiff. When the sorbet is ready place it in a sealed plastic container in the freezer.

Boil the reserved tea to reduce to a syrup for the sauce. To serve, spoon a pool of tea syrup on to each plate, place a honey basket on top and fill with the sorbet. Add a poached peach to the basket together with small bundles of redcurrants or raspberries. If liked, dust with a little icing sugar. Place a small mint sprig on top of each peach.

Puddings

MIRIAM KARLIN

Melon Surprise

SERVES 4

*T*ake a Cantaloupe melon, slice off the top and scoop out the seeds. Make up a lime jelly to a stiffish consistency and pour into the melon. Replace the top and put into the fridge to set. When set, peel the melon, and entirely cover with cream cheese, or crème fraîche, or a mixture of both, adding a little sugar or liquid sweetener and some ground ginger or liqueur to taste. Decorate with glacé cherries or strawberries and slice down into wedges.

My good wishes to Oak Lodge School. Blessings to all pupils and staff.

Hope you enjoy it !

Miriam Karlin

THE RT. HON. MARGARET BECKETT MP

*W*hilst I actually enjoy cooking, I am afraid it is something that I rarely have time for these days and so I have a couple of very quick and easy snacks that I sometimes 'fall back on'. I hope they will be of use.

I was very interested to learn of the work of Oak Lodge School and can only applaud the dedication of the teachers and parents who obviously manage under difficult conditions. It is so important to provide continuity of support and assistance to children with learning difficulties and autistic features. I wish you every success in the continuation of your work.

Bananas in Kirsch

SERVES 4

Slice the bananas and arrange in 4 individual dishes.

Sprinkle over each banana 1 tablespoon kirsch, 1 tablespoon sugar and 1 tablespoon cream.

Margaret Beckett

4 bananas
4 tablespoons kirsch
4 tablespoons sugar
4 tablespoons double cream

Puddings

Bananas in Foil

SERVES 4

4 bananas

15g/¹/₂oz butter

brown sugar, to taste

1 vanilla pod, cut into 4 pieces

1 cinnamon stick, broken into 4 pieces

1 orange, peeled and segmented

1 grapefruit, peeled and segmented

1 tablespoon grapefruit juice

1 tablespoon orange juice

1 tablespoon lemon juice

mint sprigs, to decorate

Recipe taken from BBC-TV's Good Top Chef

Peel the bananas and slice lengthwise. Butter 4 × 25cm/10in squares of kitchen foil and place a banana in the centre of each. Sprinkle with the sugar and add a piece of vanilla pod and cinnamon stick to each. Scatter over the fruit segments.

Drizzle over the fruit juices. Fold over the edges of the foil to make puffed but tightly sealed parcels.

Lay the parcels on the barbecue grid and heat through for 10–12 minutes. Take the hot parcels to your guests and cut them open at the table so that everyone can fully appreciate the wonderful aroma. Decorate with mint sprigs.

Tarte au Citron

SERVES 8

500 g/1 lb 2 oz sweet shortcrust pastry

9 eggs

390 g/13¹/₂ oz caster sugar

finely grated zest and juice of 5 lemons

250 ml/8 fl oz double cream

Recipe reprinted from Wild Food from Land and Sea, published by Ebury Press

A lemon tart cannot be served straight from the oven as the middle will still be quite runny. It needs to rest and set for at least an hour and should then ideally be served warm. However, it also tastes good cold a day later.

Lemon tart is served in my restaurant with a frozen parfait ice cream called chilboust, and a small lemon soufflé as an Assiette Citron.

Preheat the oven to 200°C/400°F/gas mark 6.

Roll out the pastry and use to line a 25 cm/10 in flan tin. Line with foil and beans and bake blind for 10 minutes. Remove the foil and beans. Check there are no holes in the pastry, and return to the oven for a further 5 minutes.

Turn the oven temperature down to 130°C/250°F/gas mark ¹/₂.

Whisk the eggs and sugar together thoroughly in a bowl, then add the lemon zest and juice. Stir in the cream.

Pour the lemon mixture into the prepared pastry case. Bake in the oven for 30–40 minutes until the filling is starting to set in the centre.

Remove from the oven and leave to rest for at least 1 hour.

Puddings

Fruit Brulée

SERVES 6–8

*N*o – Dorien never cooks!

De-seed the grapes, cut in half and put in the bottom of an oven-proof dish. Drain all the juice from the canned fruits, slice and arrange in the dish.

Crush the ratafias or amaretti and sprinkle on top of the fruit.

Spread the crème fraîche over the top and chill overnight.

Sprinkle with the sugar and place under a hot grill until the sugar is melted and bubbling. Chill again.

Enjoy!

¹/₂ bunch of grapes
1 can of lychees
1 can of mango
1 can of peaches
175 g/6 oz ratafias or amaretti
1 large tub of crème fraîche
75 g/6 oz demerara sugar

Puddings

ERNIE WISE

Cherry Delight

1 large tin of cherries
300 ml/10 fl oz double cream
500 ml/18 fl oz cherry yoghurt
demerara sugar

*D*rain and stone the cherries, and place in a shallow dish.
Beat the cream and add the yoghurt. Pour the mixture over the cherries. Sprinkle thickly with sugar to cover the top and leave overnight in the fridge. (This will form a caramel topping).

Raspberries may be used instead of cherries.

ERNIE WISE

Ice Cream

300 ml/10 fl oz double cream
2 tablespoons icing sugar
2 tablespoons brandy or coffee
2 egg whites

*B*eat the cream until thick and add 1 tablespoon of the icing sugar and 1 tablespoon of the brandy or coffee. Beat well again. Add the remaining liquid and sugar. Beat the egg whites until stiff but not dry and fold into the mixture with a metal spoon. (Fruit and nuts may be added at this stage if desired.) Place in the freezer until firm. There is no need to stir during the freezing period.

Puddings

Fruit Tart

SERVES 4

Roll out two-thirds of the pastry to a rectangle about 35 × 10cm/ 14 × 5 in. Brush with beaten egg. Roll out the remaining pastry to 2 strips about 35 × 5 cm/14 × 2 in. Place on the long sides of base, pressing to seal and form a rim. Allow to rest for 20 minutes.

Preheat the oven to 200°C/400°F/gas mark 6. Bake the pastry case on a baking shelf for 30 minutes or until golden-brown. Cool on a wire rack.

Meanwhile, make the pastry cream: whisk the egg yolks and sugar in a bowl until thick and pale. Mix in the flour. Bring the milk to the boil in a heavy pan. Whisk in the egg yolk mixture and mix well.

Return to a clean pan and bring slowly to the boil, stirring constantly. Add a few drops of vanilla essence or the ground pod.

Remove from the heat and pour into a bowl. Allow to cool.

Pipe the pastry cream down the centre of the baked pastry base. Arrange fruit over the cream and finish with a few swirls of pastry cream.

My daughter told it to me and says it works, but she's only 8!

250 g/10 oz puff pastry
1 egg, beaten, to glaze

For the pastry cream
500 ml/18 fl oz milk
4 egg yolks
100 g/4 oz caster sugar
50 g/2 oz plain flour
vanilla essence or half a vanilla
    pod, ground.

For the topping
fresh fruit such as strawberries,
    kiwi fruit, oranges, bananas,
    plums, apricots (whatever's in
    season)

*M*ay I take this opportunity to wish you every success with the fundraising for Oak Lodge School.

Apple and Cinnamon Slice

SERVES 8

For the Sponge
175 g/6 oz self-raising flour
1 teaspoon baking powder
a pinch of salt
100 g/4 oz caster sugar
100 g/4 oz butter or margarine
1 egg, beaten
175 ml/6 fl oz milk

For the topping
3–4 medium eating apples
$^1/_2$ teaspoon ground cinnamon
  or mixed spice
1 tablespoon clear honey, to
  glaze

Preheat the oven to 200°C/400°F/gas mark 6. Grease and line a 20 cm/ 8 in square cake tin with greased greaseproof paper.

Sift the flour with the baking powder and salt. Stir in the caster sugar and rub in the butter or margarine. Combine the egg and milk and mix into the flour mixture until it forms a smooth batter. Pour into the prepared square cake tin.

Core, peel and thickly slice the apples, then press the slices lightly into the mixture in the tin. Sprinkle the cinnamon or mixed spice over the apple slices. Bake in the oven for 40–45 minutes or until the sponge is springy and firm to touch.

Using a pastry brush, brush the top of the cake evenly with the honey to glaze the apples. Remove from the tin while still warm and serve warm or cold.

Yours Sincerely

Jeffrey Archer

Apple and Rhubarb Almond Sponge

Preheat the oven to 180°C/350°F/gas mark 4.

Put the apples and rhubarb into a saucepan with the orange zest and juice, sugar and sultanas. Simmer for about 15 minutes then pour into a greased ovenproof dish.

Make the sponge topping: cream the butter with the sugar. Beat in the eggs and almond essence. Fold in the flour, ground almonds and salt.

Add a little milk to give a dropping consistency, then spoon over the fruit and sprinkle the top with flaked almonds.

Bake in the oven for 30–35 minutes or until the sponge is well-risen. Serve hot with custard or cream.

450 g/1 lb cooking apples, peeled and sliced
450 g/1 lb rhubarb, cut into 2.5 cm/1 in pieces
grated zest and juice of 1 orange
75 g/3 oz demerara sugar
50 g/2 oz sultanas

For the sponge topping
75 g/3 oz butter
75 g/3 oz sugar
2 eggs
a few drops of almond essence
75 g/3 oz self-raising flour
25 g/1 oz ground almonds
a little milk
salt
25 g/1 oz flaked almonds

Farmhouse Apple Pie

SERVES 4

For the pastry
100 g/4 oz margarine
100 g/4 oz lard
225 g/8 oz plain flour
iced water

For the filling
3 large Bramley cooking apples
ground cinnamon
sugar

Make the pastry: place the fats and flour in a mixing bowl and with your fingertips rub together until the mixture resembles fine breadcrumbs, lifting all the time to allow air to enter. Then use enough water to bind together, remembering not to allow it get too wet. Place in the refrigerator to chill.

Preheat the oven to 200°C/400°F/gas mark 6.

When the pastry is chilled, roll out half of it and use to line a 20 cm/8 in flan dish. Peel and core the apples and slice them into the dish until you have it filled very well. Sprinkle with cinnamon and sugar to taste. roll out the remaining pastry and use to cover the top. Prick the pastry with a fork. Bake in the oven until the pastry is golden brown.

Puddings

Mascarpone and Lime Torte

Preparation Time: 15 minutes plus 30 minutes chilling

SERVES 6–8

Mix together the crushed biscuits and melted butter and press into the base of an 18 cm/7 in spring-sided or loose-bottomed cake tin.

Place the mascarpone, icing sugar, lime zest and juice in a bowl and beat together. Spread over the biscuit base. Chill for 30 minutes

To decorate, melt the chocolate as per pack instructions. Wash and pat dry some fresh rose leaves. Pull the underside of the leaves along the melted chocolate until coated. Allow leaves to dry coated side up.

Meanwhile, to frost the grapes, dip in water, shake off excess and coat with caster sugar.

Then carefully peel away each rose leaf starting at the stem and arrange with the grapes on top of the torte.

200 g/8 oz pack ginger snap biscuits, crushed
50 g/2 oz butter, melted
2 x 250 g tubs mascarpone cheese
40 g/1 $\frac{1}{2}$oz icing sugar, sifted
finely grated zest and juice of 2 limes

To decorate
50 g/2 oz deluxe dark chocolate
50 g/2 oz caster sugar
a few grapes

PHILIP SOMERVILLE

My Favourite Bread and Butter Pudding

Preheat oven to 190°C/375°F/gas mark 5.

Decrust the bread, and butter generously. Butter the inside of a 10 cm/4 in deep square or oblong ovenproof dish. Cut bread and butter to fit dish, and line the base with a layer of bread and butter, face up. Sprinkle mixed fruit over bread, then sprinkle with sugar. Continue in layers until you reach the top of the dish, finishing with a generous helping of fruit and sugar.

Break eggs into a jug, add milk, sherry and allspice, and beat. Pour over pudding and top with grated nutmeg.

Bake in the middle of the oven for 40 minutes. Move to the top shelf to brown for a few minutes. Serve immediately.

large white loaf
150 g/6 oz mixed dried fruit
150 ml/$\frac{1}{4}$ pint amontillado sherry
6 twists allspice
150 g/6 oz butter
110 g/4 oz white sugar
3 medium eggs
720 ml/1 $\frac{1}{4}$ pints full cream milk
nutmeg

Puddings

Cheese Cake

Ingredients:
- 600 grams Philly Cream cheese
- 4 eggs
- 6 oz. Sugar
- 1 Tablespoon lemon juice
- a pinch of grated lemon rind
- 1 Tablespoon of vanilla
- 6 Hob Nob biscuits

Crust:
Butter the pan. Crumble the biscuit in your hand. Sprinkle the biscuit into pan. Sprinkle a bit of nutmeg into tin. This will be the crust.

Filling:
Mix cheese, eggs and sugar til smooth. Pour mixture into pan. Cook in medium heat (300°F) for 40 minutes. Top of cake. will go golden in colour. Let cake cool to room temp., Then chill in Fridge. Then.....
Flip your cheese cake onto a plate.

serve - eat - Be Happy!

Peach Melba

SERVES 8

*M*ake the sauce: purée the raspberries and sugar in a food processor. Add the liqueur and chill or use immediately.

In a single serving dish, place half a peach, cut side up. Top the peach with a scoop of vanilla ice cream and pour some of the raspberry sauce on top. Serve immediately.

raspberry sauce
1 x 300 g/10 oz pack frozen
  raspberries, defrosted
2 tablespoons sugar
3 tablespoons raspberry liqueur
  (optional)

1 x 450 g/16 oz can of halved
  peaches, well drained (or
  fresh pitted peaches if
  available)
1 litre/1¾ pints vanilla ice
  cream

Chairman's Pudding

SERVES 4–6

*P*reheat the oven to 150°C/300°F/gas mark 2.
Pour the milk and cream into a saucepan and bring to the boil. Whisk the egg yolks, eggs and the sugar together. Then add the hot milk and cream mixture and blend. Strain into a bowl.

Sprinkle half the sultanas into the bottom of a medium ovenproof dish. Cut the bread slices into diagonal quarters. Arrange in the dish, overlapping each layer until the dish is filled, placing small cubes of butter on the bread. Pour the egg mixture over the bread and sprinkle with remaining sultanas.

Place the dish in a deep baking tin half filled with warm water. Cook in the oven for about 50 minutes or until golden brown.

575 ml/1 pint milk
575 ml/1 pint whipping cream
26 g/1 oz caster sugar
4 egg yolks, size 2
100 g sultanas
1 small loaf of white bread,
  medium sliced (about 16
  slices), crusts removed
65 g/2½ oz butter

Raspberry Sauce

Purée and sieve 200 g/7 oz fresh raspberries. Bring to the boil 75 g/3 oz sugar and 75 ml/2½ fl oz red burgundy with a slice of lemon rind. Add raspberry purée and reduce for about 3–4 minutes.

Apricot Sauce

Blanch, skin and stone 250 g/9 oz of ripe apricots. Purée in a blender with 7 tablespoons of sugar syrup (boil equal amounts of water and sugar for 3–4 minutes). Stir in 2 teaspoons of fresh lime juice.

These sauces can be served warm or cold.

Puddings

Rhubarb Crumble Cake

SERVES 4

For the cake
175 g/6 oz self-raising flour
a pinch of salt
100 g/4 oz butter
$^1/_2$ teaspoon vanilla essence
1–2 tablespoons milk
2 eggs
100 g/4 oz caster sugar
450 g/1 lb rhubarb, cut into
    2.5cm/1 in pieces

For the topping
100 g/4 oz self-raising flour,
    sifted
75 g/3 oz butter, cut into pieces
75 g/3 oz caster sugar

*P*reheat the oven to 180°C/350°F/gas mark 4. Grease and flour a 22.5 cm/9 in spring-form tin.

Make the topping: place the flour in a bowl and rub in the butter until the mixture resembles coarse crumbs. Add the sugar. Put aside.

Make the cake: sift the flour and salt on to a plate. Cream the butter with the sugar until light and fluffy. Mix the eggs and vanilla and add to the creamed mixture a little at a time, beating well after each addition. Add a little flour to the last addition. Add the remaining flour and the milk, blend well.

Spoon the mixture into the prepared tin and spread out evenly. Cover with the rhubarb and sprinkle over the topping.

Bake in the oven for 1 hour. Allow to cool in the tin, then remove and dust with icing sugar.

Spotted Dick and Real Custard

This good old-fashioned steamed pudding harps back to British traditions of nursery food. It is a warming golden sponge studded with currants, best served with lots of piping hot custard.

Make the spotted dick: cream the butter and sugar together until smooth. Add the grated citrus zest and lemon juice. Stir in a little of the flour at a time, alternating with a little egg until you have a smooth batter. (You could do this in a food processor.) Coat the currants in the tablespoon of flour and stir into the mixture.

Pour into a very well-buttered 1 litre/1¾ pint pudding basin and cover with a sheet of pleated greaseproof paper and foil, secured by a rubber band. Place in a pan with 3.5cm/1½ in simmering water in the bottom and steam for 1½ hours.

When cooked, run a sharp knife around the pudding before inverting on to a plate.

Make the custard: place the milk in a pan and heat. Add the vanilla and sugar. Slake the cornflour with a little water and add, stirring until the sugar has dissolved. Strain the eggs through a sieve into the milk mixture, stirring continuously until thickened. Do not allow the mixture to boil. You can keep the custard warm for up to 1 hour by placing it over a pan of hot water, with a piece of clingfilm placed directly on to the surface of the custard to prevent a skin from forming.

For the spotted dick
150 g/5 oz butter, softened
100 g/4 oz caster sugar
grated zest and juice of ½ lemon
grated zest of ½ orange
150 g/5 oz self-raising flour
3 large eggs, beaten
75 g/3 oz currants
1 tablespoon plain flour

For the custard
570 ml/1 pint full cream milk
1 teaspoon vanilla essence
4 tablespoons caster sugar
1 teaspoon cornflour
2 eggs and 1 egg yolk, beaten

Bread and Butter and Cinnamon Pudding

SERVES 4

slices of white bread
softened butter
175 g/6 oz sultanas
2 eggs
3 tablespoons sugar
570 ml/1 pint milk
1 small tin of evaporated milk
1 cup soft white breadcrumbs
1–2 tablespoons soft light
  brown sugar
2 teaspoons ground cinnamon

Preheat the oven to 140°C/275°F/gas mark 1.

Butter a deep basin. Lavishly butter as many slices of white bread as you need to fill the dish. Sprinkle plenty of sultanas between each layer of bread.

Beat the eggs and sugar together with a little of the milk. Add the evaporated milk and the remaining milk, or as much as you need to fill the dish. Pour the mixture over the bread and leave to soak for 30 minutes.

Mix the breadcrumbs with the sugar and cinnamon. Spread the mixture over the top of the pudding and cover with kitchen foil.

Cook in the oven for 1 hour. Remove the foil and cook at 150°C/300°F/gas mark 2 for 30 minutes or until the pudding is risen and brown.

DAWN FRENCH

Mars Bar Fondue

Melt three Mars Bars in a bain-marie, dip cubes of fruit or marshmallows into the mixture, on fondue sticks. Delicious!

ANITA HARRIS

Anita's Nice Ice

Gently melt some Mars Bars. Then take some Vanilla Ice Cream and pour the melted sauce over it.

I'm delighted to share this favourite family recipe with everyone connected with the Oak Lodge School, and I wish your recipe book every success. I hope you enjoy it! It's wicked, but delicious.

Puddings

Hot Fudge Sauce

*T*his recipe is for fudge sauce, which is wonderful when poured over ice cream, or as a sauce for a banana split!

75 g/3 oz soft light brown sugar
2 tablespoons golden syrup
25 g/1 oz margarine
4 tablespoons unsweetened
  evaporated milk

Place all the ingredients in a small, heavy saucepan, and heat gently for about 5 minutes until well blended together. *Do not boil.*
  Serve on top of ice cream, straight from the pan!

Puddings

Cakes,
Breads
& Biscuits

Coconut Lime Cake

SERVES 8

*P*reheat the oven to 170°C/325°F/gas mark 3.

For the cake, start off by grating the zest of the 2 limes on to a small saucer, then cover that with clingfilm and set on one side. Next measure the desiccated coconut into a small bowl, then squeeze the juice of the limes and pour this over the coconut to allow it to soften and soak up the juice for an hour or so.

To make the cake, just take a large, roomy bowl and sift in the flour, lifting the sieve up high to give the flour a good airing. Then simply throw in all the other ingredients, including the lime zest and soaked coconut, and, with an electric hand-whisk switched to high speed, whisk everything till thoroughly blended – about 2–3 minutes.

Now divide the mixture equally between the two prepared tins, smooth to level off the tops and bake on a middle shelf of the oven for 30–35 minutes or until the centres feel springy to the touch. Allow the cakes to cool in the tins for 5 minutes, then turn them out on to a wire rack to cool, carefully peeling off the base papers. They must be completely cold before the icing goes on.

To make the icing, begin by removing the zest from the limes – this is best done with a zester as you need long, thin, curly strips that look pretty. Then, with your sharpest knife, remove all the outer pith then carefully remove each segment (holding the limes over a bowl to catch any juice), sliding the knife in between the membrane so that you have the flesh of the segments only. This is much easier to do with limes than it is with other citrus fruits. Drop the segments into the bowl and squeeze the last drops of juice from the pith.

Now sift the icing sugar in on top of the limes a little at a time, carefully folding it in with a tablespoon in order not to break up the lime segments too much. When all the sugar is incorporated, allow the mixture to stand for 5 minutes, then spread half of it on to the surface of one of the cakes and scatter with half the lime zest. Place the other cake on top, spread the rest of the icing on top of that and scatter the rest of the zest over. Then place the cake in the fridge for 30 minutes to firm up the icing before serving.

© Delia Smith 1993; recipe reproduced from
Delia Smith's Summer Collection, published by BBC Books

---

175 g/6 oz self-raising flour
175 g/6 oz caster sugar
175 g/6 oz soft margarine or
   butter
3 size 1 eggs, lightly beaten
50 g/2 oz desiccated coconut
2 level tablespoons dried
   coconut milk powder
zest and juice of 2 limes
1 rounded teaspoon baking
   powder

for the icing
225 g/8 oz icing sugar
3 limes

you will also need
2 x 20 cm (8 in) sponge tins,
   4 cm (1 ½ in) deep, the base
   lined with silicone baking
   parchment

Apple Fruit Cake

100 g/4 oz plain flour

$1/4$ teaspoon bicarbonate of soda

1 teaspoon ground mixed spice

$1/2$ teaspoon ground coriander

100 g/4 oz wholemeal flour

100 g/4 oz margarine

175 g/6 oz soft, light brown sugar

2 eggs

150 g/5 oz each of currants and raisins

grated zest of 1 lemon

50 g/2 oz mixed peel (optional)

50 g/2 oz cooking apples, coarsely grated

Preheat the oven to 180°C/350°F/gas mark 4. Grease and line a 20 cm/8 in round, deep cake tin with greased greaseproof paper.

Sift the plain flour, bicarbonate of soda and spices into a bowl and mix in the wholemeal flour.

Cream the margarine and sugar in a separate bowl, and beat in the eggs, one at a time, following each with a spoonful of the flour mixture.

Fold in the remaining flour, the dried fruits, lemon zest, mixed peel, if used, and apples.

Spoon into the prepared tin, level the top and bake just below the centre of oven for about $1\frac{1}{4}$ hours or until a skewer inserted into the centre comes out clean. Remove the cake from the oven and allow to settle in the tin for about 10 minutes before turning out on to a wire rack.

PAT RAFTER

Another old favourite that Pat's mother Jocelyn makes for him.

Chocolate Supreme Cake

125g/4 oz butter

$1\frac{1}{4}$ cups caster sugar

2 eggs

$2/3$ cup plain flour

$2/3$ cup self-raising flour

$1/3$ cup cocoa

$1/2$ cup sour cream

$1/2$ cup water

Preheat the oven to 190°C/350°F/gas mark 5.

Grease the base and sides of a deep 23 cm (9 in) round cake tin. Cover the base with paper and grease the paper.

Beat butter, sugar and eggs until light and fluffy. Sift flours and cocoa together. Mix sour cream and water together. Stir flour mixture and cream mixture into butter, sugar and eggs in alternate batches.

Spread into prepared pan and bake in the oven for about 50 minutes or until firm. Stand for 10 minutes before turning on to a wire rack to cool. Leave cake upside down for decorating.

Cakes, Breads & Biscuits

Coconut Cointreau 'Mareana'

Preheat the oven to 175°C/325°F/gas mark 3.

Beat the egg white and ½ cup of the sugar to a stiff consistency. Beat the yolks with the rest of sugar until light and fluffy. Add the yolk mixture to the egg whites. Add the nuts and gently fold in the coconut, 1 cup at a time.

Pour the batter into a greased 23 cm/9 in spring-form baking tin. Bake for 45 minutes until lightly browned. Prick the cake and pour over the orange juice and cointreau mixture. Chill before serving.

6 eggs, separated
1 cup of sugar
1 cup of walnuts or pecans, chopped coarsely
2 cups of shredded coconut
³/₄ cup of orange juice
¹/₄ cup of cointreau

if desired –
1 cup of whipping cream
grated bitter chocolate to garnish

MRS SIMON REISS

Almond and Lemon Torte

Preheat the oven to 175°C/325°F/gas mark 3.

Beat the egg whites until stiff and set aside.

Beat the yolks with the sugar. Add the ground almonds and lemon zest. Fold in the whisked egg whites.

Pour the mixture into a greased and floured spring-form cake tin. Bake for 1 hour.

A few minutes before removing the cake from the oven, make the glaze: beat together the egg yolk, juice, sugar and lemon zest. Put into a saucepan and bring to the boil, stirring constantly until the mixture thickens. Add the margarine or butter.

With a cocktail stick, make a hole in the top of the cake so that the glaze can soak in when the cake has cooled slightly. Pour the mixture over and allow to stand for a few minutes. When completely cold remove from tin and chill.

For the cake
7 eggs, separated
³/₄ cup of sugar
2 cups of coarsely ground almonds
rind of 1 large lemon

For the glaze
1 egg yolk
¹/₂ cup of lemon juice and the grated zest of 1 lemon
¹/₂ cup sof ugar
1 teaspoon margarine or butter

Cakes, Breads & Biscuits

Dark Chocolate Cake

175 g/6 oz butter

6 eggs, separated

1¹⁄₂ cups sugar

1¹⁄₂ cups self-raising flour

1 tsp baking powder

1 cup drinking chocolate powder

a dash of rum

For the icing

50 g/2 oz butter

175 g/6 oz soft brown sugar

grated zest and juice of 1 orange

50 g/2 oz plain chocolate

50 g/2 oz icing sugar, sifted

50 g/2 oz plain chocolate

Preheat the oven to 180°C/350°F/gas mark 4.
Grease and line a 20cm/8in cake tin with greased greaseproof paper.

Cream the butter, egg yolks and sugar together until well blended. Add flour, baking powder and drinking chocolate.

In a separate bowl, beat egg whites until stiff. Slowly fold into the mixture and add rum.

Pour into the prepared tin and bake for 1 hour until firm to the touch. Allow to cool in the tin for a few minutes, then turn out on to a wire rack and leave to cool completely.

Make the icing: put the butter, sugar and orange zest and juice into a saucepan and heat gently until dissolved. Remove from the heat and stir in the chocolate. Continue to stir until melted. Add icing sugar and beat until of a spreading consistency.

Split the cold cake in half and sandwich together with half the icing. Spread the remainder on top.

Put the chocolate to decorate in a plastic bag in hot water. When melted, snip off a corner of the bag and drizzle the chocolate in patterns over cake.

To the Oak Lodge school Sweeties
much love
+ good luck
Joanna Lumley

Cakes, Breads & Biscuits

Carrot Cake

16–20 SERVINGS

*P*reheat the oven to 180°C/350°F/gas mark 4. Generously grease a 32.5 × 22.5 cm/13 × 9 in baking tin.

Combine the sugar, oil, eggs and vanilla in a large bowl and blend well, using a wooden spoon. Stir in the flour, cinnamon, bicarbonate of soda and salt and mix well. Fold in the carrot, coconut, pineapple and walnuts.

Pour into the prepared tin. Bake for about 50 minutes or until a skewer inserted into the centre comes out clean. Allow to cool in the tin for 5 minutes, then turn on to a wire rack and leave to cool completely.

Make the frosting: combine the cream cheese, butter, milk, vanilla and salt in a medium bowl and blend well, using an electric mixer. Beat in enough icing sugar to give a spreadable mixture. Frost the top and sides of the cake.

400 g/14 oz sugar
350 ml/12 fl oz vegetable oil
3 large eggs
2 teaspoons vanilla essence
350 g/12 oz plain flour
2 teaspoons ground cinnamon
2 teaspoons bicarbonate of
   soda
1 teaspoon salt
225 g/8 oz shredded carrot
175 g/6 oz flaked coconut
1 x 500 g/1 lb 2oz can of
   crushed pineapple, drained
100 g/4 oz walnuts, chopped
   (optional)

For the frosting
175 g/6 oz cream cheese at
   room temperature
100 g/4 oz butter, melted
50 ml/2 fl oz milk
2 teaspoons vanilla essence
$1/2$ teaspoon salt
350 g/12 oz icing sugar

I'd like to send a big hello and I do hope my recipe for Carrot Cake gives you as much pleasure as it gives me – and none of the cavities.

Maureen Lipman

Madeira Cake

75 g/3 oz butter
150 g/5 oz margarine
300 g/10 oz sugar
25 g/1 oz glycerine
2 teaspoons vanilla essence
a dash of lemon juice
5 eggs
225 g/8 oz plain flour, sifted
50 g/2 oz self-raising flour, sifted
a little extra sugar, to finish

Preheat the oven to 190°C/375°F/gas mark 5.
Grease and line 2 × 450 g/1 lb loaf tins.

Cream the butter, margarine and sugar in a mixing bowl until light and fluffy. Beat in the glycerine, vanilla and lemon juice. Gradually beat in the eggs, adding a little of the flour after each addition, then fold in the remaining flour.

Turn the mixture into the prepared tins and smooth the surfaces. Sprinkle with a little sugar. Bake in the oven for about 1 hour or until a skewer inserted into the centre of the cakes comes out clean.

Allow to cool in the tins for a few minutes, then turn on to a wire rack and leave to cool completely.

Ronnie Corbett

Cakes, Breads & Biscuits

Mocha Cake

*P*reheat the oven to 180°C/350°F/gas mark 4.

Melt the chocolate in a heatproof bowl over a pan of gently simmering water, then stir in the milk and coffee granules. Allow to cool slightly.

Cream the margarine, sugar and potato until light and fluffy. Gradually beat in the eggs and the melted chocolate mixture. Sieve the flour, cocoa and baking powder together and fold into the mixture.

Divide the mixture between two greased 20 cm/18 in sandwich tins. Bake in the oven for 25–30 minutes or until springy and firm to the touch. Allow the cakes to stand for 2–3 minutes before turning on to a wire rack. Leave to cool completely.

Make the filling: dissolve the coffee granules in the water. Put the butter, dissolved coffee and potato into a bowl and add the cocoa and icing sugar. Beat until smooth.

Use half the filling to sandwich the cakes together and spread the remainder on top. Decorate with the walnut halves.

3 tablespoons milk
50 g/2 oz plain cooking
  chocolate
1 teaspoon coffee granules
175 g/6 oz soft margarine
175 g/6 oz caster sugar
100 g/4 oz cold mashed potato
50 g/2 oz cocoa powder
1 teaspoon baking powder

For the filling
1 teaspoon coffee granules
1 teaspoon water
75 g/3 oz butter, softened
50 g/2 oz cold mashed potato
25 g/1 oz cocoa powder, sifted
250 g/9 oz icing sugar, sifted

To decorate
walnut halves

Mrs Atwood's Calla Lilies

MAKES APPROXIMATELY ONE DOZEN

These are simple to make, unusual and delicious. My mother got the recipe in the Annapolis Valley in the 1930s. Perfect for afternoon tea.

For the dough
2 eggs
$^1/_2$ cup sugar
$^1/_2$ cup flour
I tsp baking powder
a pinch of salt

For the filling
$^1/_2$ cup whipping cream
$^1/_2$ tsp sugar
$^1/_2$ tsp vanilla
grape jelly

Preheat the oven to 210°C/400°F/gas mark 7.

Beat the eggs and gradually add the sugar. Add the flour, baking powder and salt, and mix thoroughly. The dough will be runny.

Drop the dough, one teaspoonful at a time, on to a greased cookie sheet. (They spread, so leave room). Bake in the oven until golden and top springs back when touched (5 to 8 minutes).

Take from the oven one at a a time with a pancake flipper. Pinch one end of each circle together to form a calla lily shape. Cool on a rack. The cookies may be made ahead of time ot this stage.

Whip cream and sweeten with $^1/_2$ tsp of sugar and $^1/_2$ tsp vanilla, or to taste.

Put a 'tongue' of grape jelly at the wide end of the lily running towards the centre. Fill centre with a blob of whipped cream.

Serve soon after filling.

Reprinted from The CanLit Foodbook, *edited by Margaret Atwood*
Reprinted by permission of the author.

Orange Crisps

MAKES 20

Crisp, melting biscuits with a marvellous scent of oranges. These keep for 1 week at room temperature in an airtight container. They may be frozen for 3 months.

150 g/5 oz self-raising flour
50 g/2 oz caster sugar
finely grated zest of 1 orange
100 g/4 oz butter, cut into
2.5 cm/1 in chunks

Preheat the oven to 180°C/350°F/gas mark 4.

Put the flour, sugar and orange zest into a bowl. Add the butter and rub in by hand or in a food processor until a dough is formed which can be gathered into a ball. Pinch off pieces the size of a small walnut and roll between the palms into little balls.

Arrange 5 cm/2 in apart on ungreased baking sheets. Take a large fork, dip it into cold water and then press down gently on the balls to form biscuits about 1cm/$^1/_2$ in thick.

Bake in the oven for 15 minutes or until pale gold in colour. Remove from the oven and immediately sprinkle with caster sugar. Transfer to a wire rack and leave to cool completely.

ARCHBISHOP OF YORK

Yorkshire Munch

This comes with my very good wishes and support for all that you are doing at the school and in particular for autistic children. I know just a little bit about this since the child of one of my own relatives turned out to be autistic. May the Lord abundantly bless all you are doing and bring success to your fundraising activities.

150 g/5 oz margarine
50 g/2 oz sugar
2 tablespoons golden syrup
175 g/6 oz quaker oats

Preheat the oven to 180°C/350°F/gas mark 4.

Cream the margarine with the sugar in a bowl.

Warm the golden syrup and add to the creamed mixture. Stir in the oats.

Pour the mixture into a 15 cm/6 in square tin.

Bake in the oven for 30–45 minutes until golden-brown. Allow to cool in the tin, then cut into squares.

Gingerbread Men

100 g/4 oz butter or margarine
225 g/8 oz plain flour
100 g/4 oz soft light brown
   sugar
1 teaspoon ground ginger
25 g/1 oz candied peel, chopped
1 tablespoon black treacle
1 tablespoon golden syrup
1 teaspoon rum
a few currants

Rub the butter or margarine into the flour. Add the sugar, ginger and peel and mix in.

Add the treacle, syrup and rum, and mix to a dough with the hands. Cover the bowl and leave to stand in a cool place for 4 hours or preferably overnight.

Preheat the oven to 190°C/375°F/gas mark 5.

Roll out the dough on a lightly floured board to a thickness of 2 mm/$\frac{1}{8}$ in. Shape into little men with currants for eyes and buttons. Arrange spaced apart on well-greased baking sheets.

Bake in the oven for about 10 minutes or until brown. Transfer to a wire tray and leave to cool completely.

These are easy to make and a perennial favourite with young children. Other shapes can be made, such as teddy bears, pigs, cats.

Norma Major

Chocolate Chip Cookies

175 g/6 oz plain flour
1 teaspoon salt
1 teaspoon bicarbonate of soda
100 g/4 oz butter, softened
100 g/4 oz firmly packed soft
   light brown sugar
50 g/2 oz granulated sugar
1 teaspoon vanilla essence
2 eggs
175 g/6 oz old-fashioned rolled
   oats
350 g/12 oz semi-sweet
   chocolate chips

Preheat the oven to 180°C/350°F/gas mark 4. Grease baking sheets.

Combine the flour, salt, and bicarbonate of soda. Beat together the butter, sugars and vanilla in a large bowl until creamy. Add the eggs, beating until light and fluffy. Gradually beat in the flour mixture and the rolled oats. Stir in the chocolate chips.

Place well-rounded teaspoonfuls of the mixture on the prepared baking sheets.

Bake for 8–10 minutes or until golden. Allow the cookies to cool on the sheets on a wire rack for 2 minutes, then transfer the cookies, spacing them well apart, to the wire rack and leave to cool completely.

Hillary Rodham Clinton

Double Chocolate Chip Cookies

MAKES 24

Preheat the oven to 180°C/350°F/gas mark 4.

Place the sugar, butter and egg yolks in a bowl and beat together. Add the flour, salt and nuts and mix until just combined. Stir in the chocolate drops/chips.

Place spoonfuls of the mixture on baking sheets, spacing them well apart, and flatten them slightly with the back of a spoon.

Bake in the oven for 12–15 minutes until still slightly soft to the touch but golden brown.

Remove from the oven and leave the cookies on the baking sheets for 2 minutes, then transfer to a wire rack and leave to cool completely before storing in an airtight tin.

225 g/8 oz golden caster sugar
225 g/8 oz unsalted butter, softened
2 large egg yolks
8oz plain flour, sifted
$\frac{1}{2}$ teaspoon salt
50 g/2 oz walnut or pecan pieces
225 g/8 oz best-quality chocolate drops/chips

Healthy Banana Fingers

225 g/8 oz wholemeal
   self-raising flour
2 teaspoons baking powder
150 g/5 oz unsweetened muesli
40 g/1 ¹/₂ oz sunflower seeds
175 g/6 oz butter
175 g/6 oz soft light brown
   sugar
4 bananas
juice of 1 lemon
1 teaspoon sesame seeds

Preheat the oven to 180°C/350°F/gas mark 4.
   Sift the flour and baking powder into a bowl and stir in the muesli and sunflower seeds.

Place the butter in a saucepan and heat gently for 2–3 minutes until melted. Add the sugar and stir for 1–2 minutes or until melted, then stir the mixture into the dry ingredients.

Press two-thirds of the crumble mixture into the base of a lightly greased and lined 20 cm/8 in square tin. Peel and slice the bananas then toss in the lemon juice and scatter over the base mixture.

Spoon the remaining crumble mixture over the top, then sprinkle over the sesame seeds.

Bake in the oven for 40 minutes. Remove from the oven and leave to cool in the tin before cutting into 16 fingers.

Cakes, Breads & Biscuits

*B*est wishes to the pupils, parents and staff of Oak Lodge School, from all at *Brides and Setting Up Home* magazine.

I hope that this fund-raising venture is a great success.

Lovers' Knots

MAKES 50

Cream the butter with the sugar. Add the vanilla, then beat in the eggs, one at a time, beating very well after each addition. Sift the flour and salt together and fold in the ground almonds. Work into the creamed mixture to form a dough, then knead lightly. Chill for 1 hour.

Preheat the oven to 200°C/400°F/gas mark 6.

Divide the dough into pieces about the size of a walnut. Lightly flour a board, and roll out each little piece of dough into a sausage shape. It should be about 20 cm/8 in long and the thickness of your little finger in the middle, but thinner at each end. Twist each piece into a pretzel shape, like a loose knot, and press the ends firmly together to make a double ring.

Arrange the knots on greased baking sheets and bake in the oven for 10–12 minutes or until pale golden. Place on wire racks and dredge thickly with icing sugar while still hot. Allow to cool completely then store in an airtight tin. Just before serving, sift more icing sugar over the biscuits.

225 g/8 oz butter, softened
4 tablespoons caster sugar
2 teaspoons vanilla essence
3 eggs
350 g/12 oz plain flour
$1/4$ teaspoon salt
6 tablespoons ground almonds
icing sugar, for dredging

Cakes, Breads & Biscuits

*E*veryone should try this book, not just because it contains stimulating and delicious recipes, but also because it will help Oak Lodge School carry on its wonderful work.

Aunt Mary's Super Soda Bread

450 ml/16 fl oz buttermilk

3 cups of wholemeal flour

3–4 tablespoons sunflower seeds

2 tablespoons sesame seeds

1 tablespoon poppy seeds

1 cup of oats

1 teaspoon sea salt

1 teaspoon muscovado sugar

2 teaspoons bicarbonate of soda

Preheat the oven to 190°C/375°F/gas mark 5.

Butter a 900 g/2 lb loaf tin.

Put half the buttermilk into a large mixing bowl. Add 2 cups of the flour and the seeds, then add the remaining buttermilk. Add the remaining flour, the oats, salt, sugar and bicarbonate of soda. Mix together with a fork. The mixture should be quite sloppy.

Pour into the prepared tin. Bake in the oven for 1 hour.

Open the oven door slightly at the end of 1 hour and leave for 10 minutes.

Turn the loaf on to a wire rack and leave to cool.

Cakes, Breads & Biscuits

Challah

(Jewish Bread)

*P*lace 1.35 kg/3 lb of the flour in a large mixing bowl. Make a well in the centre. Sprinkle the salt around the edge.

Put the sugar into the well and add the yeast, oil, eggs and water. Mix, adding the remaining flour slowly, until the dough comes off the hands cleanly. Allow the dough to stand in a warm place for 45 minutes.

Grease 3 x 900 g/2 lb loaf tins.

Place the dough in the tins and shape as desired. Brush with egg yolk. Allow to stand for a further 15 minutes.

Preheat the oven to 140°C/475°F/gas mark 9.

Bake in the oven for about 30 minutes until risen and golden brown.

2.25 kg/5 lb plain flour
2 tablespoons salt
$^1/_2$ cup of sugar
50 g/2 oz fresh yeast
1 glass of oil
2 eggs, beaten
2 glasses of lukewarm water
2 egg yolks, to glaze

I send together with my recipe the expression of my deep admiration to the Oak Lodge School – it's reputation is second to none and being very involved with Helpline Families who do have to cope with autism, I am so happy to have the opportunity to say to you all 'Well done' – may you go from strength to strength.

With Best Wishes

LADY AMELIE JAKOBOVITS

Bara Brith

450 g/1 lb mixed dried fruit

175 g/6 oz soft light brown sugar

300 ml/10 fl oz warm strained tea

450 g/1 lb self-raising flour

1 teaspoon ground mixed spice

2 tablespoons marmalade

1 egg, beaten

Place the fruit and sugar in a mixing bowl. Pour over the tea and leave to soak overnight.

Preheat the oven to 180°C/350°F/gas mark 4. Grease a 900 g/2 lb loaf tin.

Sift the flour and mixed spice and warm the marmalade. Add the flour, marmalade and egg to the soaked fruit. Mix well, pour into the prepared tin.

Bake in the oven for 1½ hours or until a skewer inserted into the centre comes out clean. Turn out on to a wire rack and leave to cool. Serve sliced and buttered.

Cakes, Breads & Biscuits

Quick Snacks
&
Light Meals

Muesli

SERVES 4

*P*lace the oats in a stainless steel bowl with the milk and the sultanas. Leave to soak for 6 hours or overnight.

Grate the unpeeled apple and add to the mixture. Add the hazelnuts, walnuts, apricots and honey.

Bind the mixture together with the grapefruit juice and stir in the citrus zest. Add the sugar and fold in the yoghurt.

Serve as required.

100 g/4 oz porridge oats
200 ml/7 fl oz fresh milk
40 g/1 1/2 oz sultanas
450 g/1 lb eating apples
50 g/2 oz roasted hazelnuts, ground
20 g/3/4 oz walnuts, chopped
40 g/1 1/2 oz dried apricots, chopped
1 teaspoon clear honey
1 teaspoon grapefruit juice
finely grated zest of 1 orange and 1 lemon
20 g/3/4 oz demerara sugar
75 ml/3 fl oz Greek yoghurt

JOHN CLEESE

Breakfast Cornflakes

*T*his is very simple to make and absolutely delicious. An alternative is to use Coca-Cola instead of milk. Add basil as required.

Buy a packet of cornflakes.

Open the cardboard box. Open the sort of plastic packet inside the box.

Pour the contents (sort of yellowy-brownish bits of things) on to a plate.

Buy a bottle of milk.

Take the top off the thin end of the bottle. Invert the bottle gently over the cornflakes, making sure that the milk does not go over the edge of the plate.

Stewed Fruit

SERVES 4

A delicious way of using up fallen apples and summer fruit on the margin of going to waste.

4 large cooking apples, peeled, cored and sliced

any leftover strawberries, raspberries, etc.

2 large tablespoons sugar

Put all the ingredients into a saucepan with 1 cm/$^1/_2$in cold water and simmer until the apples have collapsed. Add more sugar to taste if necessary. Chill and eat on breakfast cereals.

Jenni Murray

Quick Snacks & Light Meals

My Favourite Pancakes

SERVES 4

*H*eat a round, flat pancake griddle slowly over a medium heat until a few drops of water added bounce on the griddle.

Meanwhile, combine the eggs with the buttermilk and bicarbonate of soda in a bowl and beat to mix well. Put the flour into a mixing bowl, make a well in the centre and gradually add the liquid with the remaining ingredients, beating well to make a smooth batter. Do not overbeat.

When the griddle is the right temperature, brush it with a little oil. Pour large spoonfuls of the batter on to the hot griddle. The pancakes will be about 5 cm/2 in in diameter and the griddle should hold 3–4 at a time. For thicker pancakes use less buttermilk, for thinner pancakes use more buttermilk.

When the pancakes puff up and are full of bubbles, turn them with a spatula to brown on the other side. Serve spread lightly with margarine or butter, stacking the pancakes as you do this, then pour maple syrup or any other kind of syrup on top of the stack. In place of syrup, sugar can be sprinkled over all. A delicious winter weekend breakfast!

(P.S. A tablespoon of wheat germ can be added to the batter for extra nourishment.)

2 eggs
350 ml/12 fl oz buttermilk
$^3/_4$ teaspoon bicarbonate of soda
225 g/8 oz wholewheat flour
$1^1/_2$ teaspoons sugar
3 tablespoons sunflower margarine
$1^1/_2$ teaspoons baking powder
$^3/_4$ teaspoon salt
a little oil, for greasing

MICHAEL WINNER

*A*ll I can give you is a rather dodgy recipe for scrambled eggs. Break the eggs into a bowl and add a very large amount of milk! Whisk them very very thoroughly. Get a frying pan ready with butter very hot and pour the eggs when they are foaming onto the butter. Turn them continually. That is how I do scrambled eggs and Ava Gardner told me when I told her of it that it was how Frank Sinatra did them too!

My kindest regards to you and to the school.

HARDY AMIES

I would love to help, but full recipes are difficult because I am helped with cooking by my sister who lives in the same village, or by domestic help from the island of St Helena. However, I send a tip for doing scrambled eggs:

You take the number of eggs in accordance with the number of participants. You put one egg on the side in its shell. The others you beat up lightly and put in thick saucepan with a big pat of butter. Cook over a not too hot a fire and stir constantly. When the eggs start to harden, take them off the fire and add the extra egg without beating it. You just stir it in and it gives the whole thing a flavour of fresh eggs, rather than of cooked eggs. Then add fresh cream to taste and of course, salt and pepper.

With best wishes to you and Jonathan.

Quick Snacks & Light Meals

LEO McKERN

Scrambled Eggs

SERVES 1

Break 2 eggs into a cup. Add salt and freshly ground black pepper.

Heat a good knob of butter in a small saucepan (not margarine) until dark brown and smoking.

Add the eggs, remove from the heat at once, and whisk with a fork. Delicious – the fastest hot dish known.

May the Oak Lodge School's ambitions prove as swift and as satisfactorily accomplished. With all good wishes.

SIR JOHN GIELGUD

Potato for Scrambled Eggs

SERVES 4

1.4 kg/3 lb potatoes, peeled
salt and freshly ground black pepper
2 large bunches of spring onions, chopped
50 g/2 oz butter, melted
300 ml/10 fl oz milk

Cook the potatoes in boiling salted water until tender. Meanwhile cook the spring onions in the milk until soft. Drain and reserve the milk. Drain and mash the potatoes, season with salt and beat in the milk until smooth and creamy. Add the melted butter and serve it with scrambled eggs.

Wishing your school every possible success.
Very sincerely

John Gielgud

SIR JAMES SAVILE

Single Man's Lunch

I can beans
I can soup

Pour into pan.
Heat and eat straight from pan.
(No washing up.)

We all send our good wishes to you for the success of the book and to everyone at the school.

DAVID DIMBLEBY

Baked Beans with Worcestershire Sauce

1 large tin baked beans previously cooled in fridge
ample doses of Lea & Perrins Worcestershire Sauce

Open baked bean tin. Pour Worcestershire Sauce over the top. Stir in with a spoon and eat from the tin.

With very best wishes to everyone at Oak Lodge School for their invaluable work.

Quick Snacks & Light Meals

ROWAN ATKINSON
MR BEAN RECIPE

Baked Beans (on toast)

*H*eat the beans in a pan until they go all bubbly. Pour over the toast, and serve.

ROSS KEMP

Puke on a Plate
(Also known as Cheese and Tomatoes on Toast)

SERVES 2

a knob of butter
4 ripe tomatoes, sliced
225 g/8 oz Cheddar cheese, grated
4 slices toast

*M*elt the butter in a frying pan. Add the tomatoes and stir for a few minutes over a low heat until softened.
    Add the cheese and allow to melt. Pour the mixture over the toast and serve immediately.

Brie en Croûte

1 whole Bavarian Brie Cheese
(1.5 kg/3½ lb)
900 g/2 lb shortcrust pastry
a little water
1 egg, beaten

Freeze the cheese overnight.

Preheat the oven to 220°C/425°F/gas mark 7.

Roll out half the pastry 5 mm/¼ in thick and 7.5 cm/3 in larger than the cheese. Place the frozen cheese on the pastry and bring up the pastry to cover the entire edges. Brush the pastry edge with water.

Roll out the remaining pastry to a circle large enough to cover the cheese. Press firmly but loosely on the edges so as to leave some air inside.

Brush the pastry with water and bake in the oven for 20 minutes. Brush the pastry with egg and bake for a further 15 minutes or until the pastry is golden-brown.

Remove from the oven and cool for 10 minutes before serving.

Note: It is important that the pastry does not have any opening on any part. The baking can be done hours before and rewarmed 15 minutes.

I wish the Oak Lodge School every success in its valuable and important work.

Sincere regards
Marcus Sieff

Quick Snacks & Light Meals

ROBERT KILROY-SILK

Apple and Cheese on Toast

SERVES 1

Toast the bread lightly on both sides. Grate the apple on to the bread, then sprinkle with the cheese. Toast under a hot grill until golden-brown and bubbling.

2 slices of wholemeal bread
1 Cox's Orange Pippin apple
100 g/4 oz mature English
   Cheddar, grated

THE RT. HON. MARGARET BECKETT MP

Cheese and Tomato Pitta Bread

SERVES 4

Slice open the pitta breads.
   Fill each one with sliced onion, tomato and grated cheese. Grill lightly.

4 pitta breads
2 onions, thinly sliced
2 large or 4 small tomatoes,
   sliced
100 g/4 oz cheese, grated

Margaret Beckett

Oxygen Tart

shortcrust pastry

Roll out the pastry, use to line a flan tin, and top with nothing at all. For special occasions, walnuts may be added, turning it into oxygen and walnut tart.

Suet and Suet

2.7 kg/6 lb suet
10.8 kg/24 lb suet
more suet
14 kg/31 lb suet
all available world stocks of suet

Chop 2.7 kg/6 lb of suet into slices. Fry, adding rolled suet, and stir. Mix the rest of the suet into a thick suet paste. Pour the fried suet over the suet paste base, and cook for 12 days. Serve topped with suet or with a suet sauce. (It doesn't really matter, no one will eat it anyway.)

Quick Snacks & Light Meals

Amphibian Relish

heavy syrup
string
flour paste
brown paper
1 toad (live)

Cover the toad in syrup and flour paste to slow it down, parcel up, and serve tied securely on the plate. Eat quickly. (It isn't very nice.)

© Terry Jones and Michael Palin

LARRY ADLER

I don't cook and depend mainly on restaurants. Years ago I did a War Bond tour with Irving Berlin. He took me to a New York delicatessen where I had, for the first time, a smoked salmon and sturgeon sandwich on rye bread. It was wonderful; my regret is, I've never been able to find it anywhere in London.

My best wishes for the continued success of your school. Please give my special regards to Jonathan Esdaile. I don't know him but his mother has written most movingly about him.

Larry Adler

VICTORIA WOOD

Best Sandwich Ever

2 slices of wholemeal bread, preferably with bits in
butter for spreading
lots of avocado, tomato, cucumber, cress
(alfalfa sprouts too if you live in one of the three places that sell them)
real mayonnaise
salt and freshly ground black pepper

*P*ut it all together.
    (Put the bread on the outside.)
Put mayonnaise and salt and pepper in the middle.
Eat it.

Victoria Wood

TERRY WOGAN

Chip Buttie

Take two thick slices of crusty white bread. Spread both slices liberally with plenty of butter.

Fill with sizzling hot, freshly fried chips.

Season to taste.

Eat immediately!

RINGO STARR

My eating habits have changed over the years and this is my favourite meal today:

1 good sized baking potato, baked in oven until done.

Vegetables of your choice – mine are cauliflower, broccoli, asparagus, mangetout and runner beans. Steam until firm (not too soft).

For seasoning my baked potato, I use extra virgin olive oil and Dr Braggs Aminos (instead of salt), plus a tablespoon of brewer's yeast.

Bon appétit, as they say in Monte Carlo, where I live!

Savoury Nut Roast

SERVES 4

50 g/2 oz walnuts, minced or ground

50 g/2 oz cashew nuts, minced or ground

100 g/4 oz brazil nuts, minced or ground

1 small onion, chopped and fried in 25 g/1 oz butter or oil

2 tablespoons wheatgerm or 1 tablespoon onion soup mix (optional)

100 g/4 oz tomatoes, skinned and sliced, or 150 ml/5 fl oz canned tomatoes, drained

2 eggs

1 teaspoon dried mixed herbs or thyme

salt and freshly ground black pepper

melted butter or oil for brushing

*P*reheat the oven to 180°C/350°F/gas mark 4.

Mix all the ingredients together well. Pack into a greased dish or tin. Brush the top with melted butter or oil.

Bake on the top shelf of the oven for 40 minutes or until brown.

Serve hot with gravy or onion sauce, greens and potatoes, or cold, sliced with salad, chips or rolls and butter.

Wyndhams Theatre.   20. 6. 94.

Paul Eddington C.B.E.

Here is a delicious Hungarian dish:

3 or 4 tablespoon of finely shredded cabbage lightly boiled and sautéed in butter.

Make a thinnish pancake batter, add the cabbage, make pancakes and then fold in some chopped ham.

Bon appetit!

Paul Eddington

Soufflé Suissesse

(Soufflés with Swiss cheese)

SERVES 4

This is an original way of serving a cheese soufflé; the cheese is not incorporated into the soufflé mixture but is used to glaze it. It is a light dish with a wonderful aroma, which had delighted diners at *Le Gavroche* since the day we opened. As they cook, the soufflés will absorb the cream and will by very rich and creamy.

Preheat the oven to 200°C/400°F/gas mark 6.

Melt 50 g/2 oz of the butter in a small saucepan over a low heat. Using a small wire whisk, incorporate the flour. Cook over a low heat for 2–3 minutes, stirring constantly.

Take the pan off the heat and leave the roux to cool slightly. Bring the milk to the boil, then pour it over the cooled roux, whisking all the time. Set the pan over a high heat and, stirring constantly, bring the mixture to the boil and cook for 3 minutes.

Take the pan off the heat and stir in the egg yolks. Season to taste with salt and pepper. Dot the surface with 1 tablespoon butter, cut into small pieces, to prevent a skin from forming. Set aside at room temperature.

Meanwhile, chill 8 round 7.5 cm/3 in tartlet tins in the refrigerator or freezer for a few minutes. Remove and immediately grease them generously with softened butter and arrange on a baking sheet.

Pour the cream into a gratin or bi-metal dish. Lightly salt the cream, then warm it gently without letting it boil. Beat the egg whites with a pinch of salt until they form stiff peaks. Pour the soufflé mixture into a wide-mouthed bowl. Using a whisk, quickly beat in about one-third of the beaten egg whites, then, using a spatula, carefully fold in the remainder. Using a tablespoon, heap up the mixture in the tartlet tins to form 8 large mounds.

Bake the soufflés in the oven for 3 minutes or until the tops begin to turn golden. Remove from the oven and, protecting your hands with a cloth, turn out each soufflé into the dish of warm cream. Sprinkle over the cheese and return to the oven for 5 minutes.

The soufflés must be taken immediately to the table; serve them with a spoon and fork, taking care not to crush them.

150 g/5 oz butter
50 g/2 oz plain flour
700 ml/28 fl oz milk
5 egg yolks
1 litre/1³/₄ pints double cream
6 egg whites
200 g/7 oz Gruyère or
   Emmental cheese, grated
salt and freshly ground white
   pepper

Pissaladière

SERVES 4

For the base

450 g/1 lb strong plain flour

20 g/³/₄ oz fresh yeast

1 wine glass of olive oil

a pinch of salt

milk

For the topping

3 large onions, sliced

2 tablespoons olive oil

4 large tomatoes, skinned and chopped or 4 teaspoons tomato purée

4 anchovy fillets

8 black olives

1 garlic clove, crushed

Make the base: Mix the yeast with a little warm water until frothy. Sift the flour into a mixing bowl. Make a well in the centre and pour in the olive oil and yeast liquid. Add the salt and knead well, adding a little milk. Allow the dough to rest until it has risen by three-quarters of its bulk.

Preheat the oven to 180°C/350°F/gas mark 4.

Make the topping: fry the onions in the oil until golden-brown. Stir in the chopped tomatoes or tomato purée.

Place the dough base on an oiled baking tray and flatten to a thickness of about 1 cm/¹/₂ in. Pour the tomato mixture over the dough and arrange the anchovies and olives on top. Sprinkle with the garlic.

Bake in the oven for about 20–30 minutes. Serve cold.

I would like to say how happy I am to be part of the effort to help the Autistic department of Oak Lodge School provide extra facilities which make such a difference to these children, and wish all those involved in this fund-raising project every encouragement and success.

Sincerely.

Quick Snacks & Light Meals

Ignace Vidal

Pissaladière

Quick Snacks & Light Meals

Susan's Salad

SERVES 2

crisp lettuce or chicory
1 banana, chopped
2 carrots, grated
2 tomatoes, sliced
a handful of raisins
cottage cheese or mild goat's
    cheese
fresh pineapple chunks or
    strawberries
6 blanched almonds
grated fresh ginger root
    (optional)

For the dressing
1 tablespoon chopped chives
    and parsley
2 tablespoons walnut oil
1 teaspoon lemon juice or cider
    vinegar
a pinch of onion salt
freshly ground pepper

*A*rrange a bed of lettuce or chicory on 2 plates. Arrange all the other salad ingredients on top.

Combine all the dressing ingredients, whisk well and pour over etc. salads.

With love and good wishes to all the pupils at Oak Lodge School, and wishing you great success with your fund-raising.

*With every good wish
and good luck*

Susan Hampshire

X

Quick Snacks & Light Meals

And a
Chutney

I do hope your recipe book is a great success. My recipe is very easy, and this year looks as though it's going to be a very good one for apples!

My best wishes to you all.

Apple Chutney

Peel and core the apples, chop roughly. Peel and chop the onions. Put all the ingredients into a large saucepan.

Bring to the boil and boil uncovered for about 4 hours or until the chutney is thick and brown. Pot while hot.

1.8 kg/4 lb windfall apples
450 g/1 lb sultanas
575 ml/1 pint vinegar
1 teaspoon ground ginger
1 garlic clove
450 g/1 lb onions
450 g/1 lb soft light brown sugar
1 teaspoon salt
$1/2$ teaspoon freshly ground
    black pepper

And a Chutney

Index